Largemouth, Smallmouth, and Close Kin

Largemouth, Smallmouth, and Close Kin

A Winchester Press
Pack-Along Guide to Bassin'

Dave Bowring

WINCHESTER PRESS
Tulsa, Oklahoma

Library of Congress Cataloging in Publication Data

Bowring, Dave.
  Largemouth, smallmouth, and close kin.

  Includes index.
  1. Black bass fishing. I. Title.
SH681.B685   799.1'758   82-1922
ISBN 0-87691-363-0   AACR2

Published by Winchester Press
1421 South Sheridan Road
P. O. Box 1260
Tulsa, Oklahoma 74101

Book design by Quentin Fiore

Printed in the United States of America

1 2 3 4 5   86 85 84 83 82

Contents

Section V   What the Experts Say

Foreword

In addition to a longstanding friendship, I feel a kinship with Dave Bowring because we both grew up and got our come-uppances angling for bass in southern Ohio. He has learned the craft well as is evidenced by every page in *Largemouth, Smallmouth, and Close Kin.*

He treats in vivid detail the finding and catching of America's three great basses, the largemouth, smallmouth, and spotted species. From small farm ponds to sprawling reservoirs, plus streams and rivers, you go with Dave and learn step-by-step how this veteran methodically seeks out and outsmarts "the big three."

Follow his "gearing up" instructions and you will get the ultimate efficiency from your fishing rigs whether they be bait-casting, spincasting, spinning, or flycasting. Dave believes a good fisherman is a good craftsman and the tools should fit the needs of the day. His advice on gearing and rigging reflects this.

Despite the fact that the basses are the most popular species pursued by American anglers, surprisingly few fishermen really know the when, where, and how-to basics of regularly catching bass through four seasons.

Read Dave Bowring's *Largemouth, Smallmouth, and Close Kin* and I predict you'll up your fun, fulfillment, and harvest as a bass fisherman no matter what part of the country you call home.

"Uncle Homer" Circle
Angling Editor,
Sports Afield

Editor's Preface
or How to Use This Book When You Should Have Seen How They Were Biting Last Week

---

If anyone can tell you how to catch black bass — more bass and bigger bass than you've been catching — Dave Bowring can. As Homer Circle remarks in his foreword, every page of this book shows that Dave has learned the craft well. Uncle Homer isn't inclined to bestow praise lightly. When he says that about a man, it means quite literally that the man is one hell of a fisherman. I'm not nearly that good at it, and you probably aren't, either, though both of us might be if we could spend as much time at it as the Circles and Bowrings of this world. We can't, most of us, and therein lies the value of a book like this.

Not only do I love to fish; I love to write, edit, and publish articles and books on the sport. But after a couple of decades of publishing, there's no denying I've become a little jaded. A lot of outdoor writers can tell you (and will, if given the slightest chance) that it isn't easy to persuade me of the necessity to publish a new manuscript on a given type of sport. Take the subject of this book, for instance. There are already several good books about bassing. I was impressed back in 1976 by the publication of *Advanced Bass Fishing*, by John Weiss. Lamar Underwood's *Bass Almanac* is excellent. And in 1980 I had the pleasure of publishing a Winchester Press book, *Roland Martin's One Hundred & One Bass-Catching Secrets*. That one is a 420-page opus that simply can't be beat as a complete guide to the methodology of improving your catch. Of course, the critical reader must bear in mind that Roland is a top-money tournament fisherman, so he has more limited options than the rest of us: He either has to know what he's talking about or go broke.

Well, then, why publish another book about bassing?

Because, until now, I don't think a really good, practical, comprehensive yet compact *handbook* has been available—something you can pack along on a fishing trip, read in the evening to the accompaniment of a cold beer, toss into a boat or car for quick reference when you need it, or delve into at your leisure, either for pure pleasure or as a fast refresher course.

The lack of really masterful (and really handy) handbooks has been a problem in connection with many outdoor activities. As an outdoorsman myself—and a fairly typical one, of the kind who needs all the help he can get—I used to bemoan the lack of compact quick-reference guides to some of my own hobbies such as backpacking, canoeing, high-country hiking, and various kinds of fishing and hunting. I was sure a lot of other people would agree, and that's why I decided to launch the series of Winchester Press Pack-Along Guides.

Frankly, the series is still in its infancy, with only a few guides published so far—and it will take years to produce all that are needed. But the popularity of the first few has already proved the usefulness of these guides, and Dave Bowring's work is a valuable addition to the list.

It won't bother me if a lot of neurotic Bowring fans buy the thing merely for an enjoyable read (and Dave says he doesn't care why you buy it, either, just so you buy it). But I hope you won't leave it at home on a bookshelf after reading it.

Pack it along on your next trip—even if it's just a two-hour drive to that reservoir that everyone says has begun producing—and you'll discover you have a quick problem-solver, a handy question-answerer, a collection of approaches that perhaps you haven't tried yet, a reminder of successful tricks you'd long forgotten.

If you've been getting skunked too often lately and figure a refresher course wouldn't hurt, thumb through this book and do a bit of reading wherever the subject of a heading looks helpful in your situation, on your kind of water, with the tackle and baits you've been using. You might want to read up on lakes and reservoirs, farm ponds, rivers and streams. (After moving to Oklahoma, I got into the bad habit of thinking that largemouth bassing was worthwhile only on still waters—until Dave Bowring set me straight.) Or delve into the passages on plant cover, fishing structure, figuring out patterns, or fishing the weather fronts—a section that may be worth the price of the book all by itself—or whatever else you need to know.

And if you have a *specific* problem or question, just look it up in the index and you'll have your answer fast, whether it's about free-spool reels or jig and eel rigs or whatever. There's even an appendix that will help you fillet your catch for better eating, and another that will take the snarls out of knottier problems.

Like the other notable anglers I've mentioned, Dave not only knows his stuff but knows how to share his knowledge, clearly and concisely. His articles on fishing, hunting, and other recreational activities have appeared in all the major outdoor magazines because, unfortunately, I can't claim to be the only editor who knows a good thing when he sees it. His books have earned quite a following, too. His book *How to Fish Streams* (another Winchester Press title, I'm pleased to say) has become a standard primer on equipment and methods for all moving-water species.

Imagine that! Until I found out about Homer Circle and Dave Bowring, I thought Rutherford B. Hayes and James Thurber were about the only Ohio boys who ever made good.

BOB ELMAN

Section I

The Black Bass of America

1

Largemouth Bass

There is a pond on the edge of a large midwestern city—which city and which state are not important—that draws me back time and again when the redwing blackbirds begin to gather nesting sticks and the wan spring sun begins to warm the shallows left barren of weed growth because of a long winter.

It is not likely, this early in the season, that I will see bass cruising the shorelines, because the creatures upon which they feed have not yet entered the shallows. Hibernating frogs are just beginning to clear their throats after a long winter buried in bottom mud, and last year's bluegill fry have a year's growth and know enough to remain just off the shallows where the pond drops into deep water.

Yet I know the bass are there. They patrol the dropoff just out of sight, their movements slowed by chilly waters that keep their metabolism at an ebb—a metabolism that will gradually quicken as spring advances. They have not yet begun to feel the urge to reproduce, so it is only raw hunger that draws them so near the shore.

This strange suspension of the rules of bass behavior carries over into my selection of baits as well. Deep runners, spinnerbaits,

Sometimes bass are found close to home. This five-pound largemouth was taken with a large streamer fly from a small pond in the landowner's backyard.

The largemouth bass is found in almost every state and throughout southern Canada. It thrives best in shallow weedy lakes or in the slow-current areas of rivers, and rarely goes beyond where rooted vegetation grows. (Photo courtesy Arkansas Game & Fish Commission)

and plastic worms must await warmer waters to be effective, but there is one simple black bait that works for me every spring. It is simple enough—just a quarter-ounce black jig dressed with a hank of black bucktail, to which I add a black Curlytail by Burke so that the flattened, sensuous tail rides above the point of the hook. The bait is clinch-knotted to the 8-pound monofilament on an open bail spinning outfit and cast parallel to shore, about twelve feet from

This young man used a purple worm to take an 11-pound largemouth from pad-infested backwaters.

dry land. The bait's weight quickly carries it to bottom where, in my mind's eye, I can see its black plastic tail waving seductively among the cover.

Tighten the line until the lure is felt, then hop the bait off bottom and crank the reel to bring the line taut. This is important because most bass, even the lethargic bigmouths of early spring, take the little jig while it settles back to bottom and the only mark of a strike is a slight tightening of the line.

A few hops and the taut line signals a taker. A strike to bury the hook and the surprised bass doggedly hugs bottom, not yet ready to fling itself above the pond as warmer water will permit it to do later. A few more moments of underwater fight and the bass comes to thumb, all green-backed and dark-eyed and firm-fleshed from a winter in a cold, clean pond. I admire the fish, either slipping it gently back into the shoreline waters or, if I need it for the table, snapping a chain stringer's clip through the membrane in its lower jaw before replacing it in the water. The newly strung bass fins in place, as surprised by the turn of events as I am pleased.

This is the bass fishing I grew up with, this meeting of the two of us along the grassy shores of some little pond in a consenting landowner's backyard. This is the fish many anglers from Florida to Maine and from New Jersey to California, consider to be the king of all freshwater gamefishes, the largemouth black bass.

To anglers used to the likes of brook trout or Atlantic salmon, the largemouth must seem plain indeed. Its broad back and muscular flanks carry no handsome spots, no splashes of red, blue or iridescent green. Yet to a dedicated bass angler, no fish more accurately means *fight* as does this fish.

The fish is called *largemouth* only by comparison with its battling cousin, the smallmouth bass. The corner of the largemouth's maw extends rearward to a point surpassing the iris in its eye, while

Quite a few really big Florida bass are taken on live shiner baits fished in water barely ankle deep. This is the time to let the fish have some fighting room while keeping the pressure on.

the mouth of the smallmouth is not quite so generous. Yet when the largemouth extends its mouth fully to engulf a meal, the maw indeed appears cavernous as the gills pump water, sucking the luckless creature into the bass's mouth.

The bass's coloration will vary greatly due to the chemical makeup of its home environment. I have caught nearly all-black bass from the depths of large reservoirs and old gravel pits, and I have taken bass just a shade or two away from pure white from lime-laced strip ponds in Kentucky and Ohio.

Generally speaking, however, most largemouth bass carry a basic green coloration, sometimes fading into a dusky brown along the dorsal surface, with the belly and underside of the head a cream to dirty white. The fish's lateral line, running along each side from mid-gill to the base of the tail, is a distinct black or very dark green color. It is from this lateral line that the largemouth gets one of its colloquial names, "Old Linesides." Other pet names include "big-mouth," "green bass," "green trout," and "hawg."

The eye of the bass is generally black in color, with no white visible. The fins at the base of the gill flaps, along the dorsal and ventral surfaces, and the large tailfin, are generally a translucent greenish color. The anal vent lies to the rear of the anal fin.

Once at home in the South, lower Midwest, and a portion of the East, today the largemouth has been introduced into virtually every state, most southern Canadian provinces, Europe, and Central and South America. And with this introduction has come a faithful army of anglers armed with all manner of rods, reels, lines, baits, and surefire tactics specifically designed to put a bend in the rod and a smile on the face.

The largemouth spawns when the waters of its pond, lake, reservoir, or river reach or surpass the magical 60-degree mark. It is then that the male bass, always the smaller of the sexes, begins

Florida's lakes annually produce some of this nation's heaviest bass. Note the hanging belly of the bass on the right, which is probably a female ripe with eggs.

prowling the shorelines in search of just the right spot to fan out a nest. The spots must be warmed by the sun, ruling out those overhung with shoreline willows and other warmth-blocking structures. The bottom must be flat, or nearly so, and the bottom material must be soft enough so the fish can use its tailfin and wide sides to hollow a shallow depression for its eggs. The spot, once found, may lie in water from one to five feet deep, depending upon clarity; in fact, nests are often very easy to see with the naked eye. They appear as round- or oval-shaped structures slightly lighter in color than the surrounding bottom. Unlike bluegills and crappies, bass will not tolerate the close proximity of other bass nests, so while the same long shoreline of ideal cover may house many bass nests,

The Wigly Squid by Lazy Ike gets down deep and offers the tantalizing action big bass often require.

no two nests will be found within fifteen feet of one another.

Once the nest is located, it's usually an easy matter to spot the bass itself (or more properly, *himself*). The male fish may be seen finning either just above the surface of the nest or in the immediate vicinity if the eggs have been introduced. If not, the fish will be just on the edge of the shallows in search of a female ripe with eggs. Once the female has been located, the male bass herds her toward his nest, nipping at her fins and nosing her flanks in his mating excitement. No less anxious to mate, the female allows herself to be moved over the nest where, after a bit of nipping and nudging, she deposits several thousand tiny yellow eggs which settle into the nest and cling to whatever bottom flotsam rests there. Soon after the male fertilizes the clutch with a cloud of milt, the female swims slowly away until once more herded to nest by another male.

Now the male bass turns true aggressor. It is his responsibility alone to guard the nest and its precious contents, and he will do it tirelessly, twenty-four hours a day for up to two weeks. Saving his strength, the male fins slowly just off the nest bottom, occasionally taking a lazy circular swim around the vicinity. Gills flared and dorsal fin erect, he will drive off all comers that might threaten his offspring.

And there are many such creatures in the pond. Ever-present panfish hover about the edges, occasionally darting in to grab a mouthful of eggs before the bass charges in to drive them back. Stealthy crayfish creep into the nest to dine on eggs until the male grabs the intruders, spitting them out disdainfully a few feet away. Fingerling bass also taunt the harried male, as do aquatic insects whose paths just happen to cross the nesting area. The male is never off guard, and the eggs develop "eyes" (the eyes of the not-yet-hatched fingerling bass are the first body features to distinguish themselves), hatch, and develop into the thick cloud of bass fry often seen hovering over the nest in late spring.

Once the bass have hatched, of course, the job of guarding them becomes even more difficult. The pond is full of creatures that would dine off the young bass were it not for the vigilant parent. Once the young fish reach the size of about half an inch, the male bass, realizing that his charges can now take care of themselves, drives them from the nesting site, dispersing them with flashing charges and a mouth not above devouring a few to drive the lesson home. Terrified, the young bass streak to any available cover, unaware that in doing so they also hide from a world of predators besides their father.

His job as guardian over, the male bass now goes on a feeding binge to make up for an abstinence as long as two weeks in duration. Insects, mice, frogs, panfish, and snakes—all are fair game for the hungry bass patrolling for a meal. Live creature or fishing lure, it makes little difference to the ravenous bass. A meal is a meal.

In midsummer, when much of this country's top bass waters simmer in the heat, the bass is no more comfortable with the temperature than are the anglers who seek him. Heat, combined with a scarcity of dissolved oxygen in the water caused by the decay of aquatic vegetation, drives the bass ever deeper in search of cooler temperatures. In May that hefty eight-pounder may have been resting under a shoreline carpet of lily pads, but come August the fish has retreated to the water's deepest areas. This, in farm ponds, may be only ten to twelve feet deep. In large lakes and reservoirs, the fish may relocate as much as thirty to forty feet below the surface where slightly cooler water makes for a more comfortable habitat.

No less a predator because of the weather, however, the largemouth still positions itself in or near some sort of cover that hides its bulk from passing prey species. August doesn't mean bass fishing stops—it merely changes from a shallow-water to a deep-water sport.

In autumn, when falling leaves carpet the shorelines and the first crisp days of October put color into woodland trees, the surface temperature of bass water cools once more, drawing the big predator out of the deep, back to the good hunting to be found along shoreline dropoffs, around brushpiles, and on the shoreline bars and points themselves. Food is plentiful here, and since the lean winter months are not far off, bass seem to sense the urgency of feeding at every opportunity.

Soon the autumn hardens into early winter, dropping the water temperature drastically and, with it, the body temperature of the

When the bass are deep, use a bait that gets down where the fish are. This heavy metal combination hung a nice largemouth. (Photo courtesy Iowa Conservation Commission)

bass themselves. As the rate of metabolism—the machinery used to change raw food into energy—lessens, so does the bass's need for great volumes of food. An occasional slow-moving minnow and perhaps a winter-lethargic bluegill is all the bass needs as he repairs once more to the great depths where the water is the warmest in the entire lake or pond. Growth drops; activity falls off. The bass once more awaits the coming of that wan spring sun and the warm rains that, every year without fail, draw the small creatures into renewed life and, along with them, the greatest predator in the pond, the largemouth black bass.

Although the largemouth bass is a warm-water fish, he's often caught by panfishermen plying grubs and ice flies through midwinter ice. Winter ice fishing, however, seldom yields many bass at one time. (Photo courtesy Illinois Department of Conservation)

2

Smallmouth Bass

Okay, I might as well admit this right now and get it out of the way: The smallmouth bass is my favorite freshwater gamefish. I'll make every attempt to give the other bass species as much emphasis in this book as I do the smallmouth, but it won't be easy. I grew up fishing an entire watershedful of streams, brooks, and rivers for this great fish, and it won't be easy to tone down my praise to a level matching the other species.

It's just that the smallmouth, in this angler's opinion, is, well, somehow *special*. It is a bit trimmer than its largemouth cousin, not quite as widely available, a much better battler on light line, and, in many places, far more plentiful and spunky for its size. Then too, it is much more often found in moving water than its larger bigmouthed brethren, and I must also admit a special fondness for fishing rivers and streams.

So bear with me, if you will. I, like you, am a bass-fishing nut. It's just that my preference runs to the river bass and its willow-lined home waters. Actually, the beginning angler, be he a youngster or an adult, could do far worse than dedicate his efforts to the

A very good river smallmouth comes to hand the certain way via a small landing net. The bass went four pounds and fell for a balsa diver plug.

smallmouth black bass. For I truly believe this fish to be king of the basses, no matter what others may claim in favor of the largemouth.

Consider the smallmouth's habitat. It is uniformly cooler and cleaner than that of the largemouth; in fact the very presence of good smallmouth angling is often evidence enough of the water's purity and moderate midsummer temperatures. Largemouth bass can live and thrive in water slightly off-color due to rotting vegetation and stagnant conditions, but not the smallmouth. It needs a good current, plenty of deep water or cooling riffles, a hard rock or gravel base for spawning, and a year-round flow of fresh water, if the fish lives in a river or stream. Should the health of the lake or stream begin to seriously deteriorate, the smallmouth would be the first to show it. Growth rates would drop off, feeding would be curtailed, and finally the smallmouth would disappear, even while the more adaptable largemouth bass went about the normal business of living. Perhaps that's why I hold the smallmouth special above all other basses, because it is more fragile.

Fishing literature generally has treated the smallmouth bass as somebody's black sheep, putting the smallie always behind the largemouth in terms of published praise and private conviction. Yet the smallmouth deserves no such treatment, for it holds its own in terms of fight, physical beauty, and, if it comes to that, its quality on the dinner table.

Consider the smallmouth's handsome looks. Leaner than its largemouth relative, the smallmouth seems to be quicker, more agile in the water. Once hooked, the smallmouth is famous for its display or multiple jumps, often leaping clear of the water three or four times before coming to hand. This is true for even little smallmouths. A favorite stream I fish, all too infrequently, offers an average size of only twelve inches for its bass, yet even these little battlers jump and rattle their gill rakers in an attempt to toss the barbs.

And when it comes to coloration, the smallmouth wins hands down. Depending in part on its home water's chemistry, the smallmouth most often sports a set of handsome, coppery bands vertically from dorsal to ventral surfaces. Similar but narrower bands radiate from the rear of the eye, giving the fish's cheeks and gill covers a jaunty look. Belly color is usually an off-white, and all fins are generally an olive shade. The eye can vary from solid black to a distinct red color, and the inside of the mouth is white.

The smallmouth black bass, as proper as that combination of descriptions sounds, could hardly fit its names any less. In the first place, it is *not* a bass at all, at least not in the true sense. Along with the largemouth and Kentucky spotted basses, it is a member of the

The smallmouth bass seeks out good current, deep water or cooling riffles, and suitable rock or gravel bottom for spawning.

sunfish family (North America's only true bass is the white bass). And as for being black, this species is black or very dark green for only a few days after hatching from the egg, then it turns to the coppery-green color it will carry for the rest of its life. And as for the term *smallmouth*, the fish's mouth is small only when compared with that of the largemouth.

Even the scientists blew it when they named this fish. Its Latin name is *Micropterous dolomieui* meaning *small fin*. In fact, the fish examined by the man who gave the smallmouth its Latin name happened to bear a deformed fin, one far smaller than that normally found on smallmouth. Yet the monicker *Micropterous dolomieui*—small fin—stuck, in spite of its obvious inaccuracy.

Smallmouth are said by many anglers to fight harder and with more flair than do their largemouthed cousins. I can just see the neck hairs on a good many bass anglers—especially those in the bass-oriented South—stand up when reading that statement, but I've found it true enough, time and time again, to say it straight out. Disagree if you will. Hell, it's disagreement that makes hot stove sessions good when winter's upon the bass lakes.

I had a particularly good, long look at the comparable striking power of largemouth versus smallmouth some years ago when invited to attend the Bass Masters Classic fishing tournament held on Percy Priest Lake just outside Nashville. Of course the major target was the lake's plentiful largemouth bass, but enough smallmouth were also around so that it wasn't too surprising when one of them glommed onto a bait intended for a largemouth.

There was a fifty-dollar daily prize offered to writers who caught the best bass of the day, so I kept my bait in the water right along with the contestant with whom I fished. We were off a point of land, where it fell off into deep water, and I was working a Dardevle spoon tipped with a pork rind strip, chunking it far out into deep water and retrieving it as close to the point's slope as I could manage.

Smallmouth water in Manitoba. Rapids between clear, clean lakes often provide sensational fishing for the somewhat finicky smallmouth.

A strike so hard it also took the rod from my hands (no exaggeration) slammed the rod tip into the water and set the freespool reel's drag to spinning. With visions of that fifty dollars dancing in my head, I snubbed the fish as hard as I could, although I never was able to raise the rod tip above horizontal. When I finally brought

Clear water, some current, and rock or gravel bottom for spawning sites are characteristic of good smallmouth streams.

the fish alongside, it turned out to be only a middlin'-sized small-mouth of about 2½ pounds, 16 inches of powerful bronze beauty with still enough zip to flash away once returned to the water. Never before—or since—have I had a bass strike the lure so hard, and that includes largemouths up to and over 10 pounds apiece. Oh, big largemouth bass will smack a lure pretty good now and then, especially at night when darkness makes them feel cocky and unafraid to show some power; but for day-in, day-out brute attacking force when a lure's to be hit, give me the bronze battler of fresh water, the smallmouth black bass.

How popular is the smallmouth? Surprisingly so. *Sports Afield* did a reader activity survey not long ago in which the readers were asked to check off the gamefish they fished for most often, and the results put the smallmouth into a high position. In some regions of the country the popularity of the smallmouth outstripped that of the largemouth bass. This was especially true in the cold-water Northeast and even the Midwest. In the responses from the South, however, the largemouth predictably picked up support, undoubtedly because the South offers little cool-water habitat so necessary for prime smallmouth growth and survival.

Smallmouth bass need water that is free—or nearly free—of sediment, chemical pollution, and even free of too much warming sunlight. As the Soil Conservation Service and similar agencies continue to channelize and otherwise denude streams of shade-giving foliage, the smallmouth's habitat will shrink. Just as the once-plentiful brook trout disappeared from eastern waters, so will the smallmouth. Additionally, the species needs well-aerated water, water that flows over and around limestone rocks, adding nutrients as well as dissolved oxygen. The bass must have aquatic insects and their nymphs, plus crayfish, minnows, and other forage, in order to live. It must have ideal and undisturbed spawning areas, small tributary creeks that add life-giving organisms and ox-

Small limestone streams in the Midwest and South yield an amazing number of bass every season.

Soil erosion has ruined more than a few top bass waters. This type of top-soil disturbance can be prevented with modern surface mining methods.

ygen, a bit of deep water in which to escape when mid-summer heat bakes the shallows and riffles dry up to mere trickles.

The smallmouth is a hardy beast, to be sure. But the continued dismantling of its environment nationwide can only result in a steady decrease in smallmouth and smallmouth bass fishing as another river is dammed, another stream is sterilized by channelization, another industry is permitted to vent its poison into rivers while the appropriate agency chooses to look the other way in favor of low-cost jobs and profitable tax bases.

You are the loser. The smallmouth is the loser. And when the local environment gets too ripe in which to live, we *all* are the losers. As a tired environmental poster of the mid-seventies once cried: Is it enough to make you sick? Isn't it enough to make you *stop*?

Many projects by the Corps of Engineers have turned smallmouth streams into slack-water reservoirs, suitable for largemouth fishing.

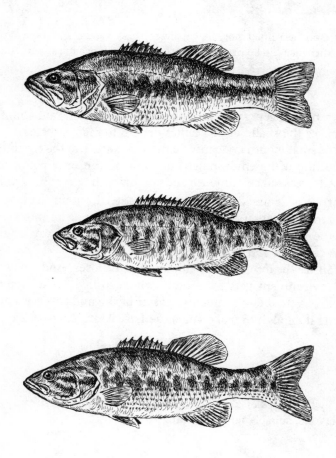

3

Spotted Bass

April on Norfork Lake, Arkansas, was as hot as August in the south of Florida. Short-sleeved arms burned and turned red under the sun, with brown spots to mark its passing when the burn finally faded. Trees in the North still wore the buds of spring, but the deep hardwoods surrounding these rugged hills were in full leaf, casting a welcome, cool shade over the deep-bottomed cuts and creeks meandering down from the heights.

We were bass fishing. Largemouths, mostly, with the odd smallmouth tossed in just to keep the attention of a visiting angler unused to such heat so early in the year. Just to escape the heat we motored inside a creek channel, its shorelines steep and falling into depths that promised to hold bass as weary of the temperature as we. And it got to be repetitive, after a while. We would motor as far as the V-bottom could navigate up the creek channel, then cut power and let the creek's gentle flow float us back to open water while we cast a then-new bait called a Road Runner into the steep shorelines. Kentucky bass, averaging about two pounds apiece,

Comparative drawings of largemouth bass (*top*), smallmouth bass (*center*), and spotted bass (*bottom*).

smacked the lures as they tumbled down the submerged hillsides. They did it with such predictability that we soon had a coolerful and began returning these chunky gamesters to the lake, once we had proved the superiority of fiberglass and monofilament line.

Since that day, I have never experienced such frantic fishing for spotted bass, and in all the time between then and now—nearly a decade—I've had time to think out *why* we caught so many good spots.

In the South, the spotted bass seeks out the deepest, coolest, and rockiest places in the lakes and streams containing the species, seemingly out-smallmouthing the smallmouth in terms of the ideal nature of its habitat. That's where we fished. The creek had carved a deep, shadowy crevice for itself, where its flow fanned into the main lake waters. The water at the bottom of this crevice was deep, perhaps thirty feet. Also present was a small but persistent current, and the creek's gouging had undoubtedly carved up quite a few rocks, all important factors in drawing and holding spotted bass.

The Kentucky spotted bass is nowhere as plentiful as are large-mouth bass in truly ideal habitat, be it in streams or lakes. In rivers and streams, there seems to be too little ideal habitat to support a burgeoning spot fishery, although the odd spot will show up in those streams holding all three bass species.

The species seems to prefer stream habitat somewhat between that sought out by the smallmouth and largemouth. While the smallmouth roams the riffles and heads of pools, and the large-mouth hangs out in slow-current areas with plenty of weeds and down timber, the spot is to be found in true backwaters, perhaps in places with stagnant water—hardly bassy-looking water to the trained but parochial eye of the largemouth or smallmouth angler.

Many spotted bass are caught by largemouth bass fishermen

The author hand-lands a smallish spotted bass from a woodland stream. Kentuckies, as they are sometimes called, can save the day when other fish are not hitting.

Spotted bass do not grow as large as either the largemouth or smallmouth; nor are they as plentiful or as widely distributed. Spots are most often found in true backwaters, including deep silted pools of sluggish, even stagnant, water. (Photo courtesy Arkansas Game & Fish Commission)

every year, clipped to the stringer, and considered to be just another largemouth. The two species do look somewhat alike, but there are quick and easy ways to tell them apart. The spotted bass always has a black spot at the base of its tail. The membrane between the soft and spiny dorsal rays is less of a true notch than in either of the other two species. Running your finger over the tongue

Places where rivers enter lakes can be real hotspots for both smallmouths and Kentucky spotted bass.

of a spotted bass will turn up a number of small but discernible teeth, a feature not found on any other bass species (save the Guadalupe bass, a bass of minor importance and not included herein).

Unless you are inordinately fortunate, you won't catch many spotted bass over four pounds in weight. Most spots, in fact, will weigh at least a full pound under that, and many only half of that. Some of the larger southern impoundments in Alabama, Louisiana, and Tennessee offer spots weighing over five pounds (Smith Lake is a good example), but with a few local exceptions, most spots are caught by anglers just bass fishing in general, rather than spotted bass angling in particular.

There is a tiny streamlet I know of, nestled covertly among the hills of a rural Ohio county. Its deepest pools seldom fall to a depth of four feet and its bottom is mostly sedimentary rock with a slick of mud here and there. Banks are lined with dense tangles of willows, and the entire stream, save a splotch of sunlight here and there, is shaded by overhanging cottonwoods, oaks, and hickories. So remote is the stream, in fact, that I have seen white-tailed deer drinking from the same pool I was fishing. We regarded each other with surprise.

The stream holds all three kinds of bass—spots, smallmouth, and a few largemouth. The first two species are easily the dominant ones, the stream being shallow and not really well suited to the largemouth's needs. The main current, barely ten feet wide in most places, is punctuated here and there with tiny sidepockets rimmed with willows, and here are found spotted bass in good numbers.

They fall for the same size and variety of artificials and natural baits that take the smallmouths, from hardware spinners to the tiniest of dry flies on gossamer leaders. They fight nearly as well, too, although they seem to prefer to do most of their battling underwater while the smallmouths put on aerial shows.

A man who has been fishing this gem of a stream for many years, Karl Maslowski of Cincinnati, showed me the water years ago for the first time, and true to my word I won't name it in print. But it does serve to illustrate that it's sometimes possible to find these not-too-plentiful fish in sufficient numbers to make for great sport.

Muskies this size and larger can and do prey on small bass where both occur, but the water tiger would rather eat carp, suckers, and other rough
fish, leaving the bass alone.

In fact, if you know of a stream holding fair to good numbers
of Kentuckies, the very best time to fish for spots can be in mid-
spring when the fish spawn. The Kentucky, like the smallmouth,
seeks out small tributary streams for its spawning run. Even the
smallest rivulets are not overlooked – I've seen spawning spots in
brooks that run bankful only in spring when runoff is plentiful;
the remainder of the year such little creeks often dry up completely
or contain only puddles.

Of interest to the Kentucky spotted bass is the tributary's gravel
beds, and it is here that the fish spawn, displaying spawning behavior much like their in-stream cousins, the smallmouth and
largemouth bass. When the little spots have hatched, they spend
the first week or so hiding and absorbing the yolk sac attached to
their bellies. Thereafter, and until they are large enough to tackle
bigger game, the little Kentuckies feed almost exclusively on tiny
insects, both aquatic and terrestrial bugs that have dropped on the
stream surface.

Larger spots, say those of a half pound or more, will take a
variety of baits, but the favorite seems to be a hardshell or softshell

crayfish fished deep and slow. Today's crankbaits, especially those with the oversize front-diving lip that causes the bait to wobble deeply and slowly, can be very effective when Kentucky bass are in deep water. Such baits as the Arbogast Mudbug and the Bomber come to mind.

I was fishing a large Alabama impoundment several years ago with a bass fisherman who had become a sort of local legend. It seemed, so the legend went, that he could catch more and bigger bass than anyone else on the lake, and I counted myself fortunate to share a boat with him—until I boated a Kentucky bass, that is.

I brought the three-pounder aboard and was about to clip it to the stringer when the legend spoke up.

"Jist a fair largemouth, son. Jist fair. They's bigger ones hyar," he said. I insisted it was a Kentucky bass, but he persisted.

"Naw, thet thar's a bigmouth, boy. Ain't no spotted bass in this lake atall," he said, spitting tobacco juice over the side.

I pointed out all the identifying characteristics of the fish I could remember. It was a Kentucky bass, sure as hell, but there was no convincing that old man. We argued back and forth and off and on for more than an hour, and that poor bass spent more time being passed back and forth between us than in the water.

When we got back to the boat dock late that evening, I was stowing my gear in the trunk of a car when I overheard the legend relating our day to a friend.

"Oh, thet boy's *nice* enough, f'sure, but he sure don't know his fish very well. Had me half-believin' he caught hisself a Kentucky spotted bass. She-it! Ain't no Kentucky bass in this here lake!"

So I just got in the car after thanking him and drove away. I suspect he still believes his beloved Alabama lake contains only largemouth bass, even if a few he catches every year *do* look a little funny next to the largemouths....

Section II

Where to Find Them

4

Lakes and Reservoirs

There are probably more magazine articles about finding bass in lakes and reservoirs than about any other single facet of bass fishing. I think this is because bass tournaments are held on reservoirs and these events get a lot of press, and because much of today's "new" bass water is in the form of dammed rivers and streams, forming new lakes and reservoirs.

Many of these articles are repetitious, to say the least. Writers with no new information to offer rehash long-established facts and fictions, and magazine editors keep publishing this stuff, perhaps sighing at the dearth of anything new on the subject.

There's a reason for all this, of course: Lakes and reservoirs are all pretty much the same, as are the bass inhabiting them. Spring finds the bass here, midsummer locates them there, and in fall they move again. Bottom structure is mentioned quite a lot, as is the temperature thermocline, dissolved oxygen, light intensity, etc. And after reading all this time and again over the years you'd probably trade your best worm rod for something, *anything*, new. Right?

Any kind of structure, whether completely below the water or partially above, has the potential of holding bass. (Photo courtesy U. S. Forest Service)

Well, I have something new to add, and you can keep your rod, old buddy.

What would you say if I told you there is a proven indicator for locating bass in virtually *any* body of water, an indicator that far surpasses oxygen content, light penetration readings, temperature, and seasonal movements as a surefire way to find bass? I mean, pinpoint them *exactly*? Well, here 'tis.

A lake's alkalinity or acidity—its pH factor—is proving to be far more important in determining the location of bass than water temperature or any other single characteristic of the water. An eight-year study done at the University of Oklahoma in Norman has revealed some amazing new facts about how bass distribute themselves in a given body of water, and what factors make them change locations. Much of what has been discovered does away with long-accepted myths of bass anglers all over the country.

Loren Hill, an ichthyologist and water-quality specialist who teaches at the University of Oklahoma, began his studies on bass behavior and water quality in 1969, using a specially designed lab test tank, a 25-acre pond, and 95,400-acre Lake Texoma on the Texas-Oklahoma border. The facts he uncovered are even now revolutionizing bass-fishing techniques.

With a handful of theories about how and why bass water quality affects bass behavior, Hill set to work in his lab. He found the available test tanks unsuited for his experiments so he designed one that permitted the creation of four distinct zones of water in one pool. The chamber is six feet long with a six-inch diameter; it is cylindrical and made of Plexiglas. Attached to it are two aspirators, known as water sources: One provides the bulk of the tank's environmental water; the other, specially prepared test water. It is the test water that alters the tank's pH, allowing Hill to observe the behavior of bass subjected to water containing various levels

Because bass are sensitive to temperature, a thermometer can help you locate them and determine how active they will be. Recent studies show that the pH of the water also affects bass behavior strongly.

of alkalinity or acidity. The pH scale runs from 0 to 14. A pH reading of 7 means the water is neutral, neither acidic or alkaline. Readings of less than 7 indicate increasing levels of acidity; more than 7 indicates alkalinity.

Hill discovered early in his testing that using several test bass measuring six inches long wasn't going to work. Invariably, one of the little bass became dominant over the others and drove them from the area of the tank containing the best pH zone. Thereafter he used only one test bass at a time. Hill said the same dominance characteristics are found in wild bass, which may explain why that hotspot you fish provides only one bass per trip instead of several. When the dominant bass is caught or leaves the area, another takes its place.

Hill found largemouth bass to be particularly susceptible to slight changes in the acidity of their environment. He theorizes that largemouth bass, like marine species, can detect changes in the pH as slight as 0.4, and that the bass will move from one location to another as the water in each spot undergoes normal fluctuations in the pH. These changes can be triggered by a number of natural causes. For example, the photosynthesis of aquatic weeds, which is greater during periods of bright sunlight, raises the pH of the nearby water. According to Hill's studies, the reason bass are found near shoreline weeds in early morning and late evening, but are absent at midday when the sun is bright, is because the weed-filled lake's alkalinity becomes too high for comfort during periods of increased photosynthesis, and *not*, as most anglers believe, because the fish react to bright light or are repelled by it. One more bass-fishing myth down the tube.

In fact, Hill took the bass's assumed reaction to bright light into consideration in his experiments. Using special light panels

Although these anglers appear to be fishing blind, they know about good bass structure on the bottom and are catching the fish to prove it. (Photo courtesy Florida News Bureau, Department of Commerce)

A fully equipped bass boat isn't a must, but it can certainly help when you have a lot of water to cover and a lot of looking to do for bass.

arranged on all sides of the test tank, Hill found that the bass distributed themselves randomly throughout the tank, rather than fleeing from bright light to darkness. From these observations, he concluded that bass do not automatically move from one light level to another. Other factors are involved, including pH, temperature, oxygen content, food, cover, and the annual spawning urge.

A reclaimed strip mine pit can support largemouth bass, provided that all acid leaks have been plugged and enough plant growth takes place to supply dissolved oxygen.

High concentrations of ammonia can lower the pH level, making the water more acidic. Rainfall with a high level of carbon dioxide has the same effect, and the introduction of large amounts of organic material into the lake (such as grass clippings or leaves) will increase the amount of carbon dioxide while lowering the dissolved oxygen level. The most important fact about all of this seems to be that pH alone is not the only environmental factor that controls bass behavior.

Feeding habits of bass were found to be greatly affected by the pH of their tank water. Hill fed his bass up to ten minnows (live) a day, and all ten were often consumed within an hour of their introduction if the water's pH was between 7.5 and 7.9, a range Hill found *ideal for bass*. If, however, the pH was lowered considerably, say to 6.7 or so, up to 60 percent of the bass either stopped feeding altogether or greatly reduced their food intake for a period of two or three days or until they became accustomed to the new water conditions. This seems to explain why changing lake conditions—heavy rain-caused muddiness, raising or lowering water levels, etc.—put bass off their feed for a time before they once again will hit a plug or take a bait. In Hill's words, bass under stress do not behave normally nor do they feed at a normal rate.

At the end of his lab studies, Hill had drawn some preliminary conclusions about how bass behavior is affected by the pH of their home water. Among these were: pH is more reliable than either oxygen content or water temperature in predicting bass behavior and movements; dominant bass take over ideal water by driving other bass away; bass feed more under ideal conditions. Hill then moved his operations outside to the 25-acre test pond to see if his theories would hold up in the cold light of on-the-water conditions.

The pond was divided into one hundred test sections on a grid pattern. Hill then selected a number of sections at random for observation. He planned to test each section for four criteria: water temperature, dissolved oxygen content, pH, and the number of bass present.

The equipment used in Hill's field experiments, in part supplied by Lowrance Electronics, was designed to record each of these factors. The boat the team used contained a fish recorder, an underwater hydrophone, and equipment needed to record all other data. A diver, swimming along the bottom to count the bass found in each section, kept in constant contact with the boat by means of the hydrophone. Hill carefully surveyed each of the randomly selected sections of the pond, and in the end he made some startling

Ohio's Dick Martin proudly displays a nice bass taken from the Santee-Cooper lakes in South Carolina. Note the plastic worm rigged with a sliding bullet sinker.

statements about the effectiveness of his method of locating bass by monitoring the pH factor.

Given the right equipment, a bass angler will find the pH method 50 percent more reliable than oxygen content for locating bass, and a full 30 percent more reliable than water temperature. Light intensity is apparently no factor at all.

Hill feels that observations made by bass fishermen for years about bass movements have been essentially correct, but the *reasons* for those movements were incorrect, and he counts himself among the mistaken group. Hill owns a fully outfitted bass boat but his lab and field research has prevented him from doing the rod-and-reel work he'd prefer.

So, the bass in your home waters react to alkalinity and acidity through their ability to control internal body fluids, extremely important for a creature that spends its entire life submerged. If the pH of a bass's body fluids varies much from their average value of 7.6, blood hemoglobin loses its ability to hold oxygen. Bass in wild environments make do with higher alkalinity levels in summer, lower levels in winter.

The behavior of bass, including smallmouth, in wild lakes, ponds, and streams should be the same as that noted by Hill in his studies. And he adds that "there is no reason why other freshwater fish, *including minnows and other bass forage species*, should not react in a similar manner." But all three environmental factors – pH, temperature, and oxygen content – influence bass behavior. "By combining these three factors," Hill says, "a fisherman can really increase his chances of finding bass."

So when you launch a boat or wade into new reservoir shallows in search of Old Linesides, you now know there's more to how bass locate themselves than the mere presence of sunken structure, an old roadbed, or some farmer's drowned fenceline. Bass know what's good for them, even if we don't, and the anglers who take the time to learn about their quarry will catch the most and the largest bass. You be one of them.

Never pass up any type of bottom cover, such as these round rocks, that might attract and hold bass in big lakes. Such spots are naturals for feeding bass. (Photo courtesy Michigan Conservation Department)

5

Rivers and Streams

Where you'll find bass in moving water, whether the water is a full-blown river, stream, or meandering woodland brook, depends in large part on the type of bass you're looking for. It isn't likely you'd locate smallmouth using the same water day in and day out with largemouth or spots, so let's look at these three species in a stream, one at a time. Locating stream bass isn't difficult if you know the habits and preferences of the fish you're after.

Smallmouth Bass

The smallmouth is a fish of moving water, water that tumbles past submerged rocks and shelves, water that's cool and contains a good supply of dissolved oxygen. In fact one of the best ways to ruin a top smallmouth fishing stream is to remove its large rocks and gravel deposits, then strip the trees from along the banks, thereby admitting hot sunlight to strike the water and raise the water temperature too much for the bass to spawn and thrive. The federal

The destruction of a bass river. A new bridge goes in and several pools in the river are dredged out. So much for progress.

and state soil conservation departments, not to mention most highway departments, seem to do an excellent job of destroying smallmouth water in just this manner.

So the water must move, and it must contain riffles as well, because riffles—especially those with a little white water—add oxygen. In midsummer, when stream water levels drop and the water heats up, look for smallmouth to congregate just downstream from large riffles. This fan of moving water contains the maximum amount of oxygen, drawing the creatures smallmouth feed on—crayfish, minnows, panfish, and aquatic insects—and the bass themselves.

During midday, and especially when the weather is hot, look for individual smallmouth to take up holding spots in relatively deep water. Just *how* deep will be determined by the overall depth of the stream and the average water temperature: the higher the temperature, the deeper the bass. Remember, all bass are cold-blooded creatures that must seek out the most ideal habitat available in order to maintain comfort. Only after comfort is met does the fish concern itself with cover, the availability of food, etc. Comfort to a bass is a matter of life and death; all else is secondary.

The bass—especially the larger ones present in a given stream —are so consistent in their choices of holding spots during warm weather that many experienced bronzeback anglers fish only known holding spots, knowing that any hefty bass around will locate themselves around these ideal places.

Harold Barefoot, a longtime fishing compadre of mine and certainly one of this country's best stream anglers, knows his home water well and can point with a rod tip to where fish will be in summer. And he'll be able to hook and boat a surprising number of these smallmouth, too. Barefoot uses only very light tackle, mostly closed-faced spin reels on 6-foot, light-action rods and 6-pound line, and a variety of ultralight lures he's found especially effective for stream smallmouth. Perhaps his most effective lure is one that has virtually no action of its own—an all-white, soft-bodied plastic

Overhanging tree cover is important because it shades the water, keeping water temperatures livable for bass during the hot summer months.

Any kind of cover – algae mats, leaves, fallen branches – may harbor bass and shouldn't be overlooked.

grub fished on a tiny eighth-ounce jig with a white head. The grub has an inch-long tail that is very flexible and that wiggles and appears to "swim" when the bait is retrieved. The grub is tossed wherever a bass might be hiding, then retrieved in a flat manner, no jigging of the rod tip or hesitation in the reel cranking. It's also important that the bait be tied directly to the line, rather than clipped to even the smallest snap swivel or other connection device. This is because the bait is so small and light that the addition of even the slightest extra weight throws the balance out of whack and makes the bait far less effective.

Other baits Barefoot finds productive are the tiny No. 00 and No. 1 Mepps spinners, using either the bronze or chrome-finish spinner blade. This bait weighs less than a quarter-ounce, but still sinks readily, so it's retrieved with the rod tip up to keep it out of bottom rocks. When the water is vodka-clear, Barefoot seems to take most of his spinner-caught bass on the bronze blade, probably because this hue sets up a more subtle flash and doesn't spook wary bass. When the water is somewhat cloudy, such as it would be following a rain, the chromed blade does a better job because it's easier for the fish to see and pursue in murky water.

Barefoot finds quite a few of his smallmouth, although seldom the largest ones, in flats of moving water where emergent rocks are plentiful and cover is therefore present. Such spots are usually rather shallow—less than three feet deep, for example—and call for a bait that floats at rest in order to avoid snags and hangups. For this he'll choose either the smallest floating Rapala, or a bait made in Ohio called the Action Certified (A.C.) Shiner, a bait similar to the Rapala (both imitate minnows), but with a blunter body and a wider variety of available finishes. Baits found to be most effective are those with a gray-colored, green-colored, or black-colored back, all three with silver-finish sides and white underbellies. These are all the Models 202 and 250 Shiners with two sets of treble hooks.

Barefoot also catches bass—and quite a few heavyweights—on any one of a variety of hard- and rubber-bodied crankbaits that sink on their own and wobble on retrieve. These are used in the deepest water around submerged cover, such as fallen tree trunks, gravel bars, and other bottom structure.

Now let's look at the specific types of places where this angler —and you too—will find smallmouth in streams. Old bridge abutments are favored locations because they offer a break in the stream current's push, as well as nooks and crannies where the fish can hide in wait for passing food creatures. Look for bass on the *downstream* side of such spots, facing upstream.

Tangles caused by two or more streamside trees collapsing in-

It's often possible to catch both smallmouth and largemouth bass from the same river pool. This angler is doing well using ultralight tackle and tiny spinners. (Photo courtesy Michigan Travel Commission)

A river spotted bass makes the water move when it feels the barb of a spinning lure.

to deep water can be very tough to fish because it's nearly impossible to get your bait in close to the fish without getting it tangled. So I suggest calling the fish out of the cover to your bait, and this means using a lure slightly larger than usual and perhaps with a bit more action and flash. Go with a bright yellow Flatfish, Tadpolly, or maybe—if you're a fly angler—an oversized streamer dressed with Mylar for a bit of flash. Wiggle and wobble the offering back and forth as close to the cover as possible, and if the bass is there and hungry, he'll zip out to inhale the offering. It then falls to you to keep him out of snags until you can thumb his jaw. I wish you luck.

Extensive beds of low-growing willows, most often found bordering that section of accelerating water just above riffles, are also home for stream smallmouth. Look for little indentations in the outside lines of willows where a crafty bass might hold while permitting the current to deliver dinner to his doorstep. Careful casting is needed here because the target pocket is small and the water shallow. It's important to cast to the rear edge of these pockets in order that your retrieve covers the maximum amount of pocket water, back to front. Don't be surprised if you get a hit the moment the bait hits the water, either; these pocket bass can be downright aggressive.

And last but not least, never pass up the mouths of feeder creeks that add fresh, cool water to larger streams. Bass congregate here both for body comfort and to feed. Toss your bait well up into the feeder creek and retrieve *with* the feeder's current into the main stream. If this doesn't work, position yourself to one side of the mouth and retrieve *across* the feeder current.

Largemouth Bass

The largemouth is not usually thought of as a stream fish, and it's certainly true that this country's heaviest bigmouths come from lakes and reservoirs and ponds, not from moving water. But to assume it's time wasted to fish for largemouth bass in streams is to pass up more action than I, for one, am prepared to do without. It's been my experience that in those streams where both smallmouth and largemouth exist, the smallmouth bass will dominate and reach the largest sizes. They will also be the most plentiful. *Usually,* that is.

Take South Carolina's Congaree River, for example. This rather slow-moving river, which feeds the Santee-Cooper Lakes, winds and meanders at an easy pace through some of the bassiest cover I've ever seen. Swamps and marshes border both sides and wide beds of lily pads and gator grass attract casts everywhere the angler looks. And here the largemouth black bass is king.

Not only is the river itself topnotch bass water—a fisherman could never leave its confines and catch all the bass he could want —there are also dozens of what natives call "blackwater pools" or ponds well back from the riverbank within the swamps and marshes. Here an angler can let his boat drift in the windless swamp (provided he knows the winding water trails from river to ponds) and fish the still water as if he were on a farm pond or tank. Cypress trunks do silent battle with gator grass and lily pads for room to grow, and the result is a plant-lined bass heaven where a man is as likely to catch a ten-pounder as he is a half-pound squirt.

The Tennessee River around Florence, Alabama, is smallmouth country where bass of eight pounds are commonly taken on emerald shiners drifted deep with the swift current. But well back from the current, where drowned swampland slows the river's drift and provides plenty of bass cover, the largemouth bass takes over and grows to a very good size. Not many people fish for bigmouths down here because the smallmouth has received all the press attention to date, but I look for the largemouth fishing here to take off in a very few seasons.

So the largemouth bass in moving water doesn't want that water to move very fast. The bass also likes his water to be relatively warm and to contain the bigmouth's usual array of food, including crayfish, frogs, minnows, rain-washed earthworms, and an occasional terrestrial insect, such as grasshoppers, beetles, and moths. The bigmouth will back back away from the current, happy to live life at a slower pace than the smallmouth. Look for him the next time you're on a slow-moving stream. He's there, just waiting.

Spotted Bass

The spot is an in-between fish, likely to be found in water not quite as swift as that preferred by the smallmouth, but yet not quite as slow-moving as that the largemouth calls home. This transitional water isn't hard to spot. Look for fans of riffle water that slow down

Obstructions, whether old dams or new, block small streams as bass highways. Spring fishing in the downstream pool, however, should provide plenty of bass action. (Photo courtesy Little Miami, Inc.)

as the channel broadens just below the riffles, or perhaps on the inside or outside of a river bend where the current changes pace, from slow to fast or vice versa. Here you'll find the Kentucky spotted bass, often in amazingly large numbers. These pockets offering great spot fishing occur because a relatively small percentage of the river is really suitable for spots, and so they gather where the living is best, even if that means a bit of crowding with their neighbors now and then.

Young spotted bass are great eaters of insects, preferring these tiny but plentiful mouthfuls even when larger prey is at hand. And this preference for insects—topwater insects, for the most part—is retained when the fish reaches its third to fifth year in the stream and has achieved catchable size, say from ten inches upward. I've found truly fabulous flyrod fishing for spots smack in the middle of a river I thought contained little save smallmouth bass. I'd be happily tossing a Wooly Worm, greased to float, or some other bushy bass bug here and there and *Smack!* I was into a spot that tried to rearrange the streambed before coming to hand. Another cast to the same location brought another topwater strike until, finally, my bedraggled bug began to sag in the current and I had to change to a fresh bait. The fish didn't care, however; if it floated and came within reach, they nailed it *right now*.

If you catch a river bass from water that looks as though it could produce both largemouth and spotted bass, how can you tell which species now hangs so prettily from your thumb? Here's an easy way, one that won't have you counting dorsal rays or going ashore to read a book: merely open the fish's mouth and run your index finger over its tongue. If the fish is a largemouth, the tongue's surface will feel mildly rough, that's all. But if that bass is a spot, you'll detect definite teeth, usually in a dime-sized cluster, on the base of its tongue. I guess the spot has tongue teeth to help crush the outer shells of the crustaceans it eats—hardshell crayfish and snails.

6

Farm Ponds

Farm ponds—called *tanks* in Texas and elsewhere in the West—produce more total bass annually than does any other type of bass water. Why? Because they are well-nigh perfect bass habitat, they are scattered nationwide and therefore available to a massive number of anglers, and quite a few state fish agencies will stock bass in private ponds provided the owner promises to allow at least some public access to the water.

Some people—probably a lot of them, in fact—are of the opinion that they can just waltz down to the pond shoreline, cast whatever's on the line at the moment, and start catching bass. It doesn't work that way.

There's a five-acre pond in a woods where I used to fish as a youngster. No one else had permission to fish the pond—in fact neither did I. Anyway, I knew the pond held bass because every once in a while I'd screw up and catch one. I didn't know much about fishing for them. The pond also held some very large carp, big red ones that had the disconcerting habit of rolling on top like huge (I thought) bass when evening stilled the waters and darkness crept closer through the woods. I was *sure* those carp were outsized bass and I wore my arm out casting every bait in the box at them, all to no avail, of course. When a companion happened to foul-hook one of these suck-faced uglies and land it, I was mortified to think I'd wasted all those evenings casting plugs to carp. You live and learn.

One way I finally managed to take the odd bass from that pond was to rig with a floating plastic nightcrawler, using no weight and dropping the bait on a carpet of lily pads shading the narrow end of the pond. I'd let the worm rest in place a few seconds, then slide it slowly off the pad it rested on, through a few inches of open water and onto another pad where it rested momentarily. The idea was to attract a bass from underneath the pads, getting it to follow the slowly moving bait until it reached the edge of the pads. Then, theory had it, the bass couldn't wait to grab the worm when it finally swam into open water out at the edge. This worked just often enough so that I got pretty smug about it, thinking I'd invented just the right method for taking sophisticated bass from a tough pond. Since then I've learned there was nothing new about the method, even though that was twenty years ago. The only thing new about it was my discovery of it. But I was cocky about my success, nonetheless. A bass is a bass.

What hung me up at the time—and prevented me from catching many bass from that or any other pond—was the idea that, because the pond was small and the fish weren't seeing much fishing pressure, the bass should be dumb and easy to catch, not to mention that I thought I could catch them at will from any part of the pond I felt like fishing. It's like hunting elephants in Illinois—you can *hunt* them, all right, but you aren't going to *find* many, on the average.

A farm pond is really just a microcosm of the sprawling bass reservoirs and lakes usually thought of as the top bass waters. The fish therein must, of course, adapt themselves to life in just a few acres of water, but that doesn't mean they don't have water temperature preferences and sensitivities to pH, weather, and the like. In short, the smart and consistently successful pond-bassing man approaches his sport with a bit of forethought. He knows the fish

Farm ponds annually provide this country's most available bass fishing. Ponds can be fished from canoes and small cartop boats, by wading, and from shore. This two-pounder hit a flyrod bug.

demand a light touch because the water is small and sensitive to disturbance. He knows that summer-clear waters permit the fish to spot shadows, and he knows a surface temperature much above 80 degrees will send the fish to the deepest lairs until darkness when they may patrol the shallows.

Let's look at some of the factors affecting pond bass. You'll be surprised how similar they are to considerations on much larger bass waters.

Structure

We think of bass structure in terms of big lakes and reservoirs, but pond bass react to bottom features just as much as their big-water cousins. If the pond you're on has an old creekbed running through it, or a fallen tree trunk across one corner of the pond, you can bet your best rod that the bass make use of such features for cover, feeding, and shade.

Quite a few ponds I've fished were constructed by heavy earthmoving equipment that found it easier to construct a bowl-shaped pond than an impoundment with sharper features. This means that the deepest water is invariably in the pond's middle and all of the shorelines are relatively uniform in slope and bottom type. Other ponds were dug in a rough V shape, with gentle shorelines falling off abruptly into an abyss of deep water perhaps as deep as 20 feet or more. These are tough to fish unless you can put a small boat on the pond and get directly over the deep water. There also are ponds around—usually they hold more good bass habitat than all others —that were built roughly parallel to the meanderings of a creekbed, and therefore contain a combination of deep and shallow water, clay banks, perhaps a gravel shoal or two, etc. Because this latter type of pond meets the needs of bass more completely, such places contain *more and bigger bass* than do the bowl and V-shaped ponds.

It's always a good idea to visit the site where a pond is being built, noting where the deep and shallow waters will be, any bottom features that might hold bass later on, and noting where the

Lily pad beds are great places to look for hefty largemouth.

outflow will be located. This is the ideal situation, but of course most of the ponds we fish have long since been completed and stocked with bass, so we have to do some brainwork if we're to become good anglers on mature waters.

It's possible to put a small boat or canoe on the pond and use a depth-finder to scan the bottom for depth. Careful use of these modern gadgets will tell you where the depths change, how abruptly they change, and what other structure, if any, is to be found there. You can also ask the landowner for information about how his pond was constructed—unless, of course, you sneaked in to fish as I did. It's not likely you'll get much help in this case—probably you'd be greeted by the muzzle of a 12-gauge.

When bass are not feeding—and this means *most* of the time, contrary to the opinion of many—they hang out where water temperature is comfortable, the pH is tolerable, and they're close enough to cover to retreat quickly should danger approach. This means bottom structure. It could be an old wooden fenceline that was left in place when the pond was filled, or it could be an old tractor body left to rust and weather. Maybe a few tree stumps lie

The author took this 6½-pounder on a May afternoon from an 11-acre farm pond. The fish hit a cork popper and required fifteen minutes from hooking to net.

just under the surface, or a clutter of logs chokes one corner of the pond. Whatever the structure is, you'll find pond bass reacting to it in much the same manner as big-water bass.

Plant Cover

Plant cover does several things for pond bass. It gives them escape cover, places to seek out baitfish and other food creatures, shade, dissolved oxygen replacement, and, I'm afraid, places to break off the angler who lets them get into deep cover in the middle of a fight. Sure, plant beds can be annoying when your oh-so-carefully cast plug plops in the middle of the bed, fouling your hooks and ruining the spot for further fishing. But plants are a very important part of every farm pond and I'll trade an occasional foul-up for the good they do.

Bass react to plants. They can't ignore them—dense plants

must be skirted, not swum through — and food fish that gain the escape of dense plants are usually lost to the pursuing bass. Plants offer shade, improved levels of acidity and alkalinity, even cover for the bass itself. And wise is the angler who, seeing plants in a pond — any kind of plants — makes them a part of his plan to catch bass.

Very often, plants (the aquatic varieties) are the only cover in a pond, and so they become doubly important. I know of a tiny puddle barely half an acre in size, in which bass cover consists only of the trunks of water willows along the banks. Bass are hardly ever found away from these trunks; in fact, the only way to effectively fish the pond is to put a small punt or johnboat on the water and cast from midpond toward shore. So tight do these fish hang in cover that a cast is useless unless it falls within half a foot of the line of willow trunks. But put that bait within striking distance of the cover — and that means within the shade line — and a strike is just a matter of time.

And let's not forget algae, that green, slimy scum that fouls treble hooks and completely covers farm ponds in midsummer in some locations. Algae, when it forms the thick, impenetrable mat scourging some ponds, cuts off sunlight and air, often killing submerged aquatic plants and thereby reducing vital oxygen. Also, if the algae-covered pond has little or no outflow during midsummer, the algae can die off faster than the oxygen depleted by its decomposition can be replaced by surviving plants. This is sure doom for the bass and all other life forms in the pond unless the water is chemically treated.

Yet *controlled* algae is a good thing, especially in those ponds lacking lily pads. Algae mats block hot sunlight, keeping water temperatures reasonable. They harbor small insects and baitfish, maintaining a steady food supply for the bass, not to mention giving escape cover to the bass themselves.

Outside Factors

Big lakes have their water skiing, power plant runoff, and paper mills. Farm ponds have outside factors that affect both the pond as a whole and the bass in particular. Let's look at a few.

Livestock can be a major disturbance on many working farms having bass ponds. Often, in fact, ponds are built for the express purpose of providing a ready water source for beef and dairy cattle, and these heavy-footed animals make daily visits to the water's edge to drink and perhaps lie in the mud tossed up under their hooves. Perhaps even more disturbing to the bass and their food system is the manure created by even a few cattle. These deposits are left in and near the water's edge, with the next rain dispersing their unwelcome nutrients to a pond already too fertile.

Farm chemicals are also problems in most locations where they are used. Pesticides poison ponds, making them as sterile as if the entire pond had been drained. Fertilizers, reaching ponds as a result of rain and other drainage systems from nearby crop fields, overfertilize a pond and can bring about its early demise, even going so far as to create a dry basin where once there was a pond. This latter is an extreme case, however, and few are the farmers who would permit such a result to occur to a valuable farm pond.

Even muskrats can damage a farm pond badly enough to destroy its ability to support bass. Muskrats use soft pond banks for their burrows and tunnels. If rainfall and snowmelt don't cause the collapse of banklines already made weak by tunnels, the heavy tred of livestock certainly will. Ponds with unwelcome muskrat populations should be trapped out immediately, if not by the farmer himself, then by local trappers who welcome the chance to add to their winter's catch of fur. Muskrats are nice to have around —*if* you don't have a bass pond on the place.

A state official discusses pollution violation with the landowner responsible. Runoff of farm chemicals into ponds and streams can kill fish directly or cause overfertilization of the waters and eventual depletion of the oxygen content.

Section III

Gearing Up

7

Baitcasting

If just one type of freshwater fishing gear has captured the minds and hearts of bass fishermen within the past fifteen years, it has to be the free-spool baitcasting outfit. No other single style of equipment spells *bass* to so many people as do these Cadillacs of the fishing world, the free-spool reels. With star drags and level winds, single and double handles, normal and souped-up gear ratios, these snazzy, modern outfits have probably accounted for more tourney winners—and more advertising dollars—than all other types of bass-fishing outfits combined.

Why? Because they are reliable, easy to use, capable of tossing nearly everything from a quarter-ounce jig and eel to a half-ounce crankbait. And do it day in and day out with only a modicum of casual maintenance and an occasional change of line.

But they're expensive, right? Well, moderately. Today's free-spool reels carry a retail price tag of between $60 and $80, admittedly no small bit of change. But consider, before opting for something less expensive and far less serviceable, that a free-spool fish-

Stickups—any type of vertical plant cover rooted in bass water—can be effective at times. Arbogast's Dick Kotis did well using baitcasting gear and sinking plugs.

ing outfit, given even the most minimum of care, will do more for you on the water, last longer, and serve the plug-caster as well as the live-bait man.

What brand reel should you choose? I'm on no tackle manufacturer's payroll and can therefore speak freely and without fear of claims that I do so out of favoritism. I prefer the Ambassadeur series of reels by Garcia (the firm has recently been purchased by its Swedish affiliate), simply because my experience to date with free-spool equipment has been with Ambassadeur reels. To date I've used the Model 5000, one of the cherry-red models with single reel handles, star drag, and level-wind features. This served very well and never gave me a moment's worry as to reliability or maintenance. Then I tried the 2500C model, an emerald-green reel with single handle, star drag, and, most importantly, an anti-reverse feature that permits the reel drag to give line *only* when the reel handle is not in hand. When I clamp down on that reel, the fish simply *cannot* gain line via the drag, a great feature when fishing for large bass in snaggy water.

In fact, my 2500C reel proved its worth to me the very first time I took it on the water. I was fishing an especially bassy 11-acre farm pond that was full of lily pads, surface algae, and an impossible tangle of downed logs and brush. The bass were there, but so were the snags. I tied on an 11-inch black plastic worm, Texas-rigged with an offset hook and a sliding bullet sinker, and dropped the worm mere inches from a brushpile I felt had to hold at least one good bass. The bait plunked down, sunk to bottom, and lay there until I twitched it off the mud. Within a minute the tip of my rod bounced, indicating a taker, and I lowered the rod tip, slowly picking up line on the green reel until it tightened against something solid out there among the snags. When the bass turned to go, I reared back on the Fenwick rod and crossed that fish's eyes.

To make a short story even shorter, the anti-slip feature of the reel permitted me to handle that bass in a manner that kept her out of the snags, and within two minutes, after several jumps and no little surface thrashing, the fish came to thumb. She weighed, some three hours later on a butcher's scale, a bit more than 6¼ pounds and remains today the record for that particular pond.

Proper equipment is the secret to successful fishing when you must enter the water after your sport. This fisherman comes equipped with waders, vest, stout tackle of the right type, and Polaroid glasses.

And I give a lot of credit to the little green reel that didn't give line when the bass tried hard to gain the protection of the brush.

The reel, of course, is really only half of the basic baitcasting outfit. The rod makes up the rest, and it's so important a half that no knowledgeable basser should downplay the magnitude of the rod's role.

The type of rod you choose, at least in part, depends on what you plan to do with it. You already know, of course, that a rod intended to toss plastic worms should be shorter and stiffer than a stick to be used for plug casting. And a rod you'll use to bounce jigs off a rocky point will differ from a rod used to fish spoons and live bait on bottom in some 30-foot hole in a bass lake. So begin by knowing to what use you'll put the rod, then begin handling all the sticks in a tackle store, just like the guys who have no idea what rod they want to buy.

Oh sure, everyone does it. All those gleaming rods, some in

fiberglass and some in graphite and maybe even a few in boron. They stand shining in all their pristine glory just begging you to grab a fistful and pay through the nose for rods that no more match the job they're to do than a Continental does a roadrace. But once you've managed to overcome the gushy urge to buy every rod on the rack, think a little about what you want that rod to do for you, and go from there. Remember, you can afford just *one*.

It stands to reason, of course, that if you intend that stick to lob plastic worms and a quarter-ounce sliding sinker, you probably won't want the rod to be too supple. Worm rods—generally under six feet long with a pretty good spine—are built like that because it matches the job at hand. Rod length is short so you can fire that fake into deep brush without hanging up in overhead foliage. The rod's spine is stiff so you can feel the tap-tap of a pickup telegraphed up the line and down the rod into your hands, then tighten the line and sock it to him. Fenwick makes a nice line of worm rods, but other brands (but not all) on the market also perform well.

If, however, you'll want that rod to cast plugs, spinnerbaits, and jigs fairly long distances, you'll want a stick with more length and a faster tip. Both of these features make day-long casting less of a chore, and you can use the natural whip of the rod tip—instead of your arm and shoulder muscles—to lay out nice long casts.

And for those baits that don't impart their own actions merely by virtue of their retrieves, the rod of course must be sensitive to every little wiggle, freefall, and pizzazz your hand can muster. And the rod must transfer the action accurately to the line and, in turn, to the bait itself. So the more sensitive the rod is without becoming too much like a limp noodle, the better off you'll be.

Now, what about the line guides and tiptop on that rod? And what type of material should the handle be, and in what style? If you don't consider these when you buy the rod, you could well be

How game is the smallmouth bass? This medium-sized fellow hit a plug nearly half its length—and got hooked. (Photo courtesy Tennessee Game and Fish Commission)

93

stuck with a piece of equipment that simply isn't fun to use – and why put up with that?

Inspect the rod closely. Check the guides, their wrappings, and how each guide aligns with its fellows. Question the store clerk about the material the guide linings are made of. Some are clearly better than others because the better ones are constructed of hard-finish alloys and chemicals that simply *do not* build up friction heat during cast, retrieve, or fight. This is especially important for the tiptop because it must withstand more – far more – pressure than the other guides. The tiptop must remain super smooth because any tiny hairline fracture or sign of wear can cause friction and heat, which will weaken the line, be it braided nylon or monofilament.

Let's say you've found just the rod for you but you aren't happy with the guides and tiptop already installed. It's certainly possible to remove the old ones and install specially purchased hard-finish models. If you don't want to tackle the job yourself, perhaps the store clerk knows of a reputable rod repair shop that will do the job for you, or perhaps a friend builds his own equipment and will install the new guides for a few dollars.

Rod handles seem to be made of almost anything the manufacturer had on hand at the time – plastic, cork, alloys, you name it. I prefer cork, however old-fashioned that sounds, because even when wet, cork is easy to grip and has just enough natural "give" to it to make a handle comfortable for day-long fishing. Not that the theory's foolproof, however. Quite recently a friend and I were fishing New Jersey's huge Lake Hopatcong and I'd just finished rigging a cork-handled rod. My hands were very dry and, on the very first cast, the rod literally jumped from my hand and plunked into seven feet of dark, weedy water. My friend made several dives trying to recover the dropped rod, but to no avail. I trust the damn thing is happy where it lies.

Lures

There's a trend in today's baitcasting lures to go smaller and lighter, undoubtedly due to the increased quality and sensitivity found in modern free-spool reels and better rod actions. This is all to the good because I'd bet my best Fenwick that most lunker bass, given a choice, will more often go for baits of a smaller size than for the grenade-sized plugs we used to be stuck with. Today's outfits can toss fluttery-bladed spinnerbaits, buzz them across the pads, and then turn around and chunk a hefty Big O bait far up the cypress channel in pursuit of the hawg bigmouth that just swirled at the base of a tree.

So we have better baits, and that means better, more comfortable fishing. It also means more fish.

Spring Baits

There are two baits that have so consistently produced bass for me in the early months that I would no more go without them than I would go without my favorite (and only) fishing hat. One is the black jig and eel, the other is the spinnerbait.

I discovered the spring-killer nature of the jig and eel quite by accident. It was the first week in April and I was with two friends fishing a rather tiny farm pond containing martini-clear water. The water was so transparent that we could see the bass before we cast to them — lying in the shadow of a submerged log, along a row of cattails, a few slowly cruising just offshore. It was enough to make a bass fisherman's rod throb. But the wind was up and virtually everything I tried tossing ended up in a curve that even Pete Rose couldn't hit. Clearly, I needed something that would cast well, even in that gale, well enough to let me pinpoint my offerings for all those delicious-looking bigmouths out there in the pond.

A bit of rummaging in the tackle box turned up a handful of black leadhead jigs weighing a quarter-ounce apiece and dressed with black bucktail. They looked promising, especially in that wind, but I wanted a bit more allure to the lure, so I dug farther. Up popped a forgotten packet of Burke Curlytail grubs, also black. The grubs, added to the jigs, put a little wiggle into the baits while permitting excellent casting. I attached one such combination with an improved clinch knot to my mono and fired a cast a few yards

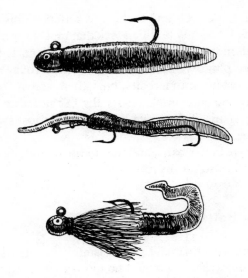

Jig-and-eel rigs are very good for taking bass in the spring. *Top*, leadhead jig with single hook and plastic body can be cast, trolled, or jigged. *Center*, a rigged artificial eel with weighted head and double hooks. *Bottom*, black leadhead jig, dressed with black bucktail and Burke Curlytail grub—the author's surefire springtime lure.

beyond a pair of bass finning beside a log. You aren't going to believe this, but it's true and I have witnesses: Both bass must have seen the lure in the air because suddenly they left cover and raced to see which of them would get to the morsel first. A fish struck just as the lure struck the water, and I was into a spring-strong bass that preferred to run and bulldog underwater rather than jump. I tried the lure again, after thumbing the bass, and caught three more fish on half a dozen casts. The black jig and eel, or jig and grub if you prefer, has been a standard spring bait for me ever since.

Of course, the success these baits can have doesn't always please everyone. One late March day, overcast and with a bit of remnant chill in the air, I took compadre Jim Robey, outdoor columnist for the Dayton *Journal Herald*, to a favorite piece of bass water of mine.

The bass weren't yet spawning, but were tight on the shorelines, feeding heavily, when we arrived. Jim broke out his favorite bait, a minnow imitation, while I went with the *black death* combination once again.

The first fish was mine, a nice five-pounder that sucked in the bait while it freefell in a few feet of water. I snapped the bigmouth to a stringer, and a second bass inhaled the bait while Jim was still looking for his first action of the day.

Without going into more detail (the above is enough to make Jim steam a bit when he reads it), by day's end I'd caught at least fifteen bass, keeping five that had a total weight of about seventeen pounds. Jim and his minnow bait had accounted for one small bass of less than a pound and a half. Those fish just *wanted* a black jig and grub, perhaps because it imitated that pond's super plentiful tadpoles that seem to swarm over all the shallows every spring. They, too, are all black and have the same tail movement imparted by the black grub.

The second spring bait that's produced handsomely for me time after time is the spinnerbait, that crazy safety-pin lure with either one or two spinner blades, a dogleg-shaped wire connector, and a firmly attached leadhead jig with a skirt of plastic, fiber, bucktail, or what-have-you.

I think the spinnerbait's major attraction—and the reason it's found in so very many tackle bins—is its versatility. The bait can be retrieved flat through open water; it can be buzzed over the surface like a baitfish or other creature trying to escape; it can be sinuously wiggled and woven in, over, and around sunken and emergent brush with enough sensuality to make even the most resistant bass come with its mouth open. The bait is virtually snagproof, too, a big help when you're after fish that try to live in the trees and in the water, all at the same time.

Why is the spinnerbait so effective, more effective, often, than the spinner-type lure using a single wire shaft to house both blade and bucktail? Perhaps it has something to do with the separation between blade and bucktail. Or maybe the simple V-shaped construction of the spinnerbait is easier to fish effectively in snaggy water, and therefore is used more often and catches more fish. I

The spinnerbait is a top lure during early spring and when largemouths are feeding on top later in the year. This angler has a scrappy three-pounder and a boxful of baits. (Photo courtesy Michigan Travel Commission)

don't know the reason, and it's not important anyway. What *is* important is that it catches bass. A lot of bass. And it does it *often*. That's good enough for me.

There is at least one alteration you can make on your store-bought spinnerbaits that's bound to make them more effective, no matter how you fish them, and that's to turn the skirt backwards. Most commercial spinnerbaits are sold with the skirt facing the hook; the skirt is rather streamlined and the best the angler can expect is a bit of flare when the retrieve speed of the bait is altered.

Turn that skirt around so that the "flare" faces up the shank, away from the hook. Rigging this way forces the skirt into a wide, seductive pattern every time the bait is moved through the water, whether buzzed across the surface or jigged slowly past some underwater bass cover. Try it; it works.

But just in case the spinnerbaits you buy don't come with sufficient skirting, several bait companies produce spare skirts in any color you could want. These are made of plastic, fibrous material, and a host of other materials, virtually all designed to go soft and seductive in the water. It's easy to change skirts on spinnerbaits, and often doing so makes them much more effective.

There's not a lot that can be said about baitcasting lines, mainly because baitcasting lines don't differ at all from those used on open-bail spin rigs or spincast outfits, except perhaps that baitcasters usually opt for lines of slightly stouter test than do the spin anglers. But one point should be made: Whichever brand of line you choose, and of whatever test, be sure you have confidence in it. I once did an outdoor column for a large midwestern newspaper and in that position received far more fishing gear, including line, than I could ever use.

One such free sample was a massive spool of lovely mono line. It was fine, except for its color: bright orange. It just didn't *look*

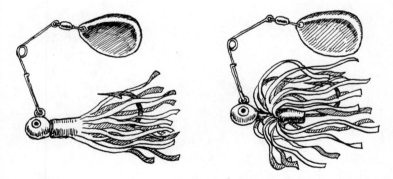

On most commercial spinnerbaits the skirt faces the hook (*left*). Reverse the skirt (*right*) so that it flares in a wide, seductive pattern when the bait is moved through the water and you'll have a more effective bait than the store-bought original.

like it would catch fish, but I spooled it up anyway and visited a local bass pond. A dozen casts later I'd had no strikes and, after another hour, firmly believed the line prevented action, so I removed it, stored it on a shelf and forgot it.

Yet less than a month later I was fishing with members of a local bass club and the topic of colored lines popped up. You guessed it: To a man, everyone there raved about this new orange line that permitted them to see as well as feel the take of a plastic worm, yet the bass seemed not to notice the line's unusually bright color. Needless to say, I trotted myself home and gave that line another shot. Caught bass, too, now that I had the confidence in the line to stay with it through slack bass-catching periods.

I ended up catching quite a few bass on that fire-engine monofilament, too. So confidence in the line – or lure, or rod, or reel – is as important as anything else in bass fishing. That's a lesson I won't soon forget.

8

Spinning and Spincasting

In terms of the number of fishermen using it, spinning and spincast equipment is the most popular type of gear going. That's understandable because it also happens to be the easiest equipment to use, requiring just a little know-how and achieving maximum casting distance with a minimum of backlash and other annoyances. Unlike either flycasting or baitcasting gear, the family of spin outfits readily adapts to the use of either live or artificial baits, certainly a major reason for its popularity.

In fact, lightweight open-bail spinning outfits have more than earned their keep at major bass tournaments across the country. Trends among serious bass anglers, especially those plying clear waters, have been toward smaller, lighter, and shorter plastic worms, and the new light spin outfits handle these baits with ease. In fact a major tourney held on massive Lake Mead was won by an angler using ultralight gear exclusively. He said following his victory that the lake water was so clear, and the bass's vision so keen, that he had to go with the cobweb line such tackle offered in order to take bass consistently. This is often true elsewhere in the country, especially on lakes and streams where bass are fished for a lot and the fish have become lure-wary. There's no better way to combat such wariness than with very fine line and small baits.

Some anglers know this, of course, and seem to catch fish when others don't, much to the consternation of their fellows. One such

chap is Harold Barefoot, a canoe manufacturer and bait dealer from Ohio. Barefoot prefers to fish with small artificial baits in the ponds and rivers near his home. (I described his favorite smallmouth lures in Chapter 5.) For stream smallmouth and largemouth bass, he'll opt for his 6-foot glass spincast rod, a quality Zebco closed-bail reel, and 6-pound monofilament line. So light is the terminal gear that no snap swivel is used—at least not a complete snap swivel. Harold uses a pair of fingernail clippers to clip off the swivel, leaving just the tiny, gossamer brass snap, which he ties to the end of his line. This assembly permits him to switch lures quickly and easily, yet so reduces the total weight that the actions of the lures he uses—spinners, balsawood plugs, and tiny jig-grub baits—are not impaired.

Fishing with Harry can be frustrating. Of course we always fish his home water, the lovely and fish-filled Stillwater River, and he always outfishes me. Flyrods, baitcasting outfits, and spinning rigs notwithstanding, I just can't seem to keep up with him. While I'm trying to unwind some errant line from the spindle of my spinning reel, he's snaking a cast here or striking a fish there. While my flyline is still in the air, Harry is thumbing the lower jaw of a nice smallmouth. The results started me thinking. Why do I continue to use outfits that take so much on-the-water maintenance while I could be fishing? I guess Harry will continue to outfish me until I store everything save a closed-bail outfit like his. It's the only way I'm ever going to win.

There is both good and bad in everything, and spincast outfits certainly are no exception. The determined bass angler wants to fish with no tackle hangups, no equipment failures, every time out. You accomplish this by buying good material, wisely, to start with. Do less and you invite disappointment.

Start with the rod. The standard spinning rod is made of fiber-

The closed-face spincasting reel offers almost the same long casts as the open-face variety, but is plagued with fewer backlashes. It's a good choice for novice anglers.

glass and is 6½ feet long from tiptop to handle butt. The handle is made of cork rings around the glass rod butt, and the reel seat is usually made of a rather cheap metal sheeting cast to house the reel foot under a threaded ring or two. Such an outfit can be expected to deliver several years of carefree use, and if you are like most of us and must settle for small- to medium-sized bass, such a rod will do fine.

There's been a lot of talk over the years about the advantages of one-piece rods over those of two or more pieces, with advocates of the former insisting that one-piece rods offer better action and a more continuous flow of power, butt to tip. I guess that's true technically, but you couldn't prove it by me. I've used both one- and two-piece rods and found them comparable in every way on the water. In fact the two-piecers travel much better because they break down into a much handier overall length. There are few things requiring more special handling than a one-piece rod, even when transported in a roomy station wagon. Put one of these dudes on small, brushy water, *then* try to put it together, and you'll quickly see the advantage of a two-piece rod. Try to get a one-piece rod of any length on and off a commercial airliner, *in good shape*, and you'll swear off the one-piecers for all time.

Now, about the rod you'll buy. If you plan to chunk plugs, spinners, and plastic worms with that spinning rod, get it with a stout tip. There are few more tiring exercises in this world than trying to spend a day casting rather heavy baits with a wet-noodle rod—it can and will wear you down in short order. Instead, get a rod with guts to it, both in the butt and out near the tip where the flex and muscle must be. Why put all the casting onus on your arm and wrist when a good rod will do part of the job for you?

Let me put in a good word for the snap cast. I've seen anglers using a sidearm motion that would make Sandy Koufax jealous,

This angler had luck using one of the oldest bass plugs, a red and white wooden popper fished on light tackle. (Photo courtesy Wisconsin Conservation Department)

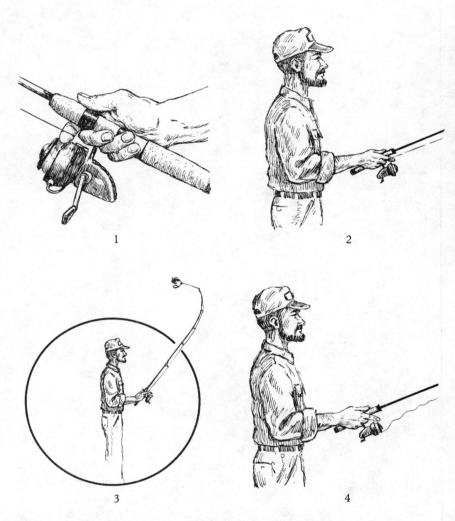

1

2

3

4

Use a snap cast to get your lure exactly where you want it without scaring the bass away. Start (1) by shortening the line between the lure and rod tip to eight inches or less, using your index finger to control the line; then (2) aim the rod forward and sight along it to a point two feet directly over your target; (3) snap the rod butt backward, stopping at the two o'clock position; finally, (4) snap the rod tip forward while simultaneously releasing the line.

and I've seen chaps using the *bomb method* of casting that threatens to reduce the size of migrating geese five hundred feet up in the air, and so have you. A fellow I know, who regularly fishes one of the largest lakes in an eastern state, is an adamant bomb-method caster. Whether using spinners or other baits, he insists on leaving at least two feet of line between rod tip and bait before every cast, then making casts that describe a perfect semi-circle through the air. I once asked him why he left so much line free before casting, and he replied that it gave him much better arcs in his casts. Now there's a chap who just doesn't know the rudiments of good casting form—or what it takes to fire a lure through dense cover after elusive fish. Long, arching casts may *look* poetic, but they seldom do the job if bass are what you're after.

In the first place, all kinds of bass, regardless of subspecies, are wary, and banging that lure on the water surface is no way to introduce the program to a bass—he'll just hightail it for the nearest cover till you're through frothing the water. And it's virtually impossible to achieve pinpoint accuracy with the bomb method—it just can't be done consistently.

Try the snap cast. This makes use of the built-in strength of that well-chosen rod of yours. Start by shortening the free-hanging line between the lure and tiptop to a maximum of eight inches, half that as you get the hang of the method. Then point that rod tip directly toward your target and sight along it at an imaginary target two feet directly over the target, right in midair. That's what you're shooting for. Then, with a snap of the wrist, buck the rod butt back toward your casting shoulder, stopping it abruptly in the two o'clock position. *As soon as the rod tip follows the rod butt back toward your shoulder, snap it forward,* aiming for that imaginary target in the air over the target water, simultaneously releasing the line by straightening your index finger or, in the case of a spincast outfit, releasing the reel button. The lure will sizzle in a flat, hard line straight at the target, and if you've judged distance versus force correctly, the lure will drop *exactly* where you want it, having at no time been more than four feet off the water's surface.

This, very simply put, is the snap cast. In most cases it's done with the rod held perpendicular to the water so you're not endangering fellow anglers with hook-impaled ears, and since it makes use of the rod's innate flexibility and recovery actions, it's easier on your shoulder than any other casting method. The snap cast is especially well suited to the spin and spincast outfits in use today, but with just a little modification it can be used with baitcasting gear as well.

The open-bail spinning idea came to this country from France following World War II, and with it a whole new era in fishing thought. No longer did the casual angler have to put up with slow-geared baitcasting outfits of the day. Now he or she could learn to use this new spinning tackle in a matter of minutes, well enough to begin catching fish immediately. The beauty of the tackle is its versatility; it does equally well with lures or baited hooks and bobbers. If that smallmouth won't hit a crankbait, maybe he'll take a live shiner minnow or nightcrawler suspended at just the right depth. Using the weight of the bait and bobber alone, spin anglers can cast effortlessly and, with a bit of practice, accurately.

There was a day on Bull Shoals Lake not long ago when it was spinning gear or nothing. The bass were in the lake's thinnest water during their spring spawn. Depth was no more than a foot at most, and even the lightest of baitcasting lines and baits made the fish swirl off the nest in alarm. My guide, a grizzle-chinned old man who'd been fishing the Shoals for years, switched to a very light spinning rod, tying on one of those cigar-shaped topwater plugs that rocks and wiggles at rest. The plug was made of balsa and although fully six inches long, couldn't have weighed more than a quarter-ounce.

The guide snap-cast the bait over the shallows, fingering the line coils skillfully to settle the bait on the shallow water as lightly as a thistledown. The bait plopped and began to wiggle; we could see the sow bass's dorsal fin less than six feet away. Slowly it turned toward the intruding cigar plug; the fin seemed to flare a bit as the bass homed in on her target.

I didn't see the fin move, but suddenly the plug disappeared into a hole in the lake the size of a kitchen table and the guide struck hard. The fish had nowhere to go so she went up, crashing back into a hard run that took her (thankfully) into deeper but snag-free water. To end this story quickly, the bass weighed a bit over nine pounds and appeared to be full of ripe eggs, so the guide carefully thumb-handled her while removing the hooks and slipped her back into the lake. She wasted no time heading back into the shallows and her temporarily abandoned nest, and the guide broke off the first five feet of line and retied the lure.

For the beginner, there is no better choice in outfits than button-operated spincast tackle, provided you steer clear of the really cheap models on the market (usually found in discount stores packaged under plastic bubbles on cardboard). Backlash free, simple to operate, and fully capable of catching good fish, spincasting tackle makes an excellent choice for children just learning to handle their own fishing gear.

My father's best intentions were sidetracked when I needed that first fishing outfit many years ago. He passed by the simpler gear for a flyrod and automatic flyreel for me. I caught a few fish with it, sure, but not half as many as a dependable spincasting outfit would have permitted. And I'd have inflicted far fewer hook wounds on him and other fishing companions with a spincaster than with that unwieldy old flyrod. My son Danny will learn on a spincast outfit—you don't think I want hooks impaling *my* head, do you?

Lures

The artificial baits available to spin fishermen virtually duplicate those for baitcasters; the only real difference is the size and weight of the lures. Spinners, spinnerbaits, floater-divers, alphabet crankbaits—all are available to the spincasting fisherman. These baits can weigh anywhere from $\frac{1}{3}$ ounce down to $\frac{1}{64}$ ounce, and can be fished in a wide variety of actions, depths, and modifications.

Take the relatively new plastic grub baits, for example. Some are nearly as large as plastic worms and need no additional weight for effortless casting. Others are tiny—less than an inch long overall—and must be fished on ultra-fine spinning lines and in virtually snag-free waters.

Serious bass fishermen have a variety of effective lures in their tackle boxes.

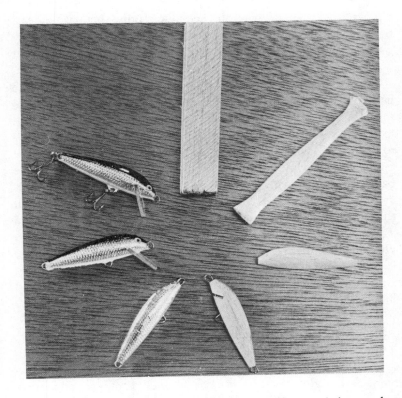

The steps in making a floater-diver Shiner plug, from raw balsa wood to finished lure. This can be a deadly plug when bass are in water no more than five feet deep.

Sports Afield Angling Editor Homer Circle heard that I was headed for Georgia quite recently in search of that state's giant redear sunfish. Gentleman that he is, Uncle Homer sent me a plastic boxful of new white grub baits weighing $\frac{1}{64}$ ounce each, including the tiny gold jigs used to rig them. "Remember," he said in an accompanying note, "these little jigs are best fished on 2-pound-test line and ultralight spinning outfits. Cast them out, let them sink to or near bottom, and use a s-l-o-w flat retrieve for those big panfish." I did as I was told, keeping in mind that bass, at least bass of any size, would hardly bother themselves with such tiny morsels, so although bass and redears inhabited the same ponds I was fishing, I wouldn't be bothered with bass while after panfish.

I was dead wrong. Not only did the bass bother with my little white grubs, they positively *loved* them. In fact, a morning's fishing turned up nine keeper bass on the little baits and only two sunfish. The bass had turned the tables and were beating the sunfish to the baits. It was touch and go, of course, because the jigs' single hooks were so tiny I had trouble keeping the steel buried in the bass's jaws, but I managed to take nine good fish up to five pounds apiece, not counting the little bass I didn't bother to count. And all this was on a 5-foot whip of a spinning rod, a Mitchell 204 reel, and 2-pound line. Ever take a 5-pound bass on line that light? You don't horse him, you just sort of *convince* him.

Worm fishermen have discovered that open-bail spin outfits, consisting of short but stiff rods, reels with good drags, and limp line, make excellent ways to fish today's shorter, lighter worms in thin water. Bullet sinkers now come in ever-smaller sizes and weights, and offset hooks, favored by wormers, also fit the smaller, lighter rigs.

In fact you'd be hard pressed to find even one serious tournament bass angler whose tackle doesn't include at least one, often more, spinning rigs. Let's face it—spinning equipment offers far too much versatility and ease of use to be ignored by people who make at least part of their living on the tourney trail. I doubt that any serious bass fisherman, even if he never attends a bass tournament, would want to be any less equipped to handle today's more and more complex bass-fishing situations.

9

Flycasting

The dark green water spreads before me, waist-deep, looking more like an odd-patterned carpet than a slough off mighty Lake Marion near Santee, South Carolina. Afloat with diatoms, bits of algae, and small beds of water lilies, open water was only an occasional thing. In chest waders and armed with an 8-foot flyrod and a wool-lined bookful of bass bugs, I was after the fabled monster bass of Russelville Flats, one of Santee-Cooper's most famous wading areas.

Fishing had been rather slow. Only two small bass had fallen for my bucktail flies. The lone keeper that showed itself by leaving a heavy swirl on the surface hadn't shown a second time and my repeated casts to the spot had drawn nothing save a huge bullfrog that followed my bug a few feet before it, too, sank from sight.

I returned to the bass boat where it was tied to a dead limb. I rested my rod on the gunwales and rummaged in a cooler under one seat. At least the beer will be cold, I thought. Suddenly, less than twenty feet from the boat, a bass swirled. I nearly dropped the beer, trying to grab the flyrod and shake loose a few coils of line before the bass left the spot. The hairbug floater swished through the air once, twice, then spatted within inches of the silvery rings left by the bass. I didn't have to move the bait at all. No sooner had it struck the water than the bigmouth came up and slurped it in, its broad tail showing clearly as it turned back for

Flyrodding for bass is catching on as more anglers discover that bass will hit flies and bugs as readily as trout will.

cover. I struck the fish hard, knowing a firm hookup would be necessary in this floating plantation of plants, stickups, and brush.

Surprised by the prick in its jaw, the bass ran a few feet against the tightening leader, then leaped clear of the surface twice. It was a good bass, maybe seven or eight pounds, and I gave only enough line to keep the 10-pound leader from parting. One more jump, a heavy wallow that threatened to take the fish far under a bed of pads, and the fish was coming my way. Despite tangling the loose coils of flyline around my wading suspenders, and nearly falling over backwards while backing away from the pad bed, I horsed the bass closer until, by reaching far out over the water, I thumbed the bass and lifted it clear of the surface. Its red-black eyes stared and its great tail waved slowly, but the thumbed jaw numbed the fish and it struggled no more as I wearily waded boatward while trying to calm nerves forever jangled by taking a heavy bass on the lightest of tackle.

Fly gear isn't the only way to catch bass, but I believe it's the most fun. Moreover, it's occasionally the *only* way to take fish consistently, even when the legions of veterans scoff at the long wand as a serious tool for bass.

There have never been a *lot* of fly fishermen in this country, not even when you count those after trout, salmon, and panfish along with the bassers. Year after year, reports by tackle manufacturers say that only ten percent of the total equipment sold in a year's time is fly-oriented, while spinning, spincasting, and baitcasting gear comprise the bulk of all tackle sales. So when I talk about flycasting for bass, I know the audience of active flyrodders is small, but that sure doesn't mean they or their sport should be ignored. In fact, to be perfectly candid, I think flycasting for bass, be they largemouth, smallmouth, or Kentucky spotteds, is one of anglingdom's highest pursuits.

For those of you who would, if asked, refuse to give up your spinning or baitcasting outfits, I would suggest you consider merely adding a flyrod and a handful of floaters to your tackle bins. These will add a whole new dimension to bass fishing and can also add bass to your catch when no other type of tackle produces.

Getting It Together

Assembling a fly outfit for bass isn't difficult but it should involve some careful considerations before any money changes hands. Start with the fish. Will it be stream smallmouth? Largemouth bass in ponds, lakes, and reservoirs? Maybe a combination of the two? The fish you're after will determine which lures you need, which in turn will help decide what size and weight rod you'll buy. In turn, that determines the line style and weight, leader material, and, to a certain extent, the size and style of the reel.

If the rod is to be used mainly for largemouth bass you'll probably want a rod capable of throwing flies of pretty considerable bulk, such as hairbugs, poppers, oversized streamers, and such. For this job you'll want a rod with a pretty stout spine, something that will turn these big baits over in the air and lay them down where the fish are—without slapping the water. Such a rod, often labeled as a bass or bug model, is usually about eight feet long and takes a line size of 7, 8, or 9. The butt section is hefty and the tip, although somewhat whippy, retains a good deal of strength to move that big package of line and lure through the air.

You'll probably end up getting a two-piece rod, and although they have their detractors, two-piecers do just fine for me and are a heck of a lot easier to transport than one-piece sticks. Now, will that rod be glass or graphite? The former is a lot more common and a lot less expensive, and it's the material I would recommend if this is your first flyrod. If, however, you have some experience with the long wand and don't mind paying at least half again as much as you would for a glass model, by all means go with graphite, or maybe one of the new boron rods.

Graphite has what the manufacturers call a fast *flex recovery*. That means graphite returns to its normal (straight) position faster than would a glass rod of similar spine and length. What that means to the angler is less muscle required to lay out a long line — the rod does most of the work while the fisherman actually just "starts" the rod action and holds it in the proper position. And don't let a graphite rod's tiny diameter fool you. The rod may *look* weak, but it has more guts than a comparable glass model. Most graphite rods are black in color, by the way, and some are brightened up with especially snazzy guide windings.

Okay, you've chosen the fish you're after and know what lures you'll have to buy or tie; and you've gotten a rod to do the job. It's now time to match the right line to that rod and this is simpler than you might think.

Flylines are numbered; the larger the number, the heavier (denser) and larger in diameter the line is. For example, a No. 9 line is far heavier than, say, a No. 5 line.

Flylines are also divided into so-called families according to the configuration of the line. A so-called level line has the same diameter along its entire 30- to 35-yard length. A weight-forward line tapers, with the greatest bulk and weight built into its forward end. A so-called bug taper line has a long belly of heavy line, and the ends of the line rather quickly taper into tips of smaller diameter line, the better to make large, bulky flyrod lures turn over in the air.

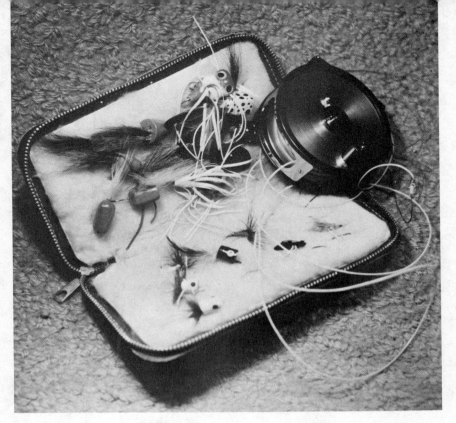

When bass are on top and feeding, topwater fly bugs can be real killers.

There are also lead-core lines designed with fast-sinking characteristics, and other specialized line rigs designed to allow superlong casting on big rivers. Such lines as these, however, seldom if ever are needed by the bass angler in everyday fishing situations.

The most important single consideration in matching a line to a flyrod is the weight of the line. All flylines worth their salt are numbered on the outside of the container. Similarly, all quality flyrods commercially produced bear a like number on the base of the rod, just above the top of the cork handle or grip. If these two numbers match, your line and rod should perform well.

The fly reel is nothing more, in most bass-fishing situations, than a line repository. It hangs under your rod, provides a bit of balancing weight, and picks up or yields line as needed to cast or fight a fish. Some models come with built-in drags, others must be

palmed when a fish is to be slowed. I would suggest buying a quality single-action reel rather than any of the automatic (spring-loaded) reels available today. It's easy enough to hand-crank a single-action reel, and these little gems have no springs to break at just the wrong time.

Bass-fishing leaders are not as all-important as those meant for trout fishing, for two reasons. First, bass are not nearly as wary of leaders and the shadows they throw, as are their cold-water cousins. Second, bass don't inhabit water that's as clear as trout streams and lakes, so the angler can get away with leaders of very moderate length and rather stout construction. I usually use a 6- to 8-foot length of level monofilament testing about 10 to 12 pounds, maybe a little finer if small poppers are to be used. In any event, I never go lighter than a 6-pound line, and I have used leaders testing as high as 17 pounds, especially in snaggy water. Remember, the bass you're after is a predator, and he will ignore or fail to see your leader if the bait on the end of it is presented and worked in a life-like manner.

Tactics That Work

It isn't very often that the flycaster after bass can rely on rising fish to mark his quarry. Bass, although they can and do feed on top extensively, are not subject to predictable timing like trout, because they don't rely as heavily on aquatic insects such as caddisflies and mayflies that are the meat and potatoes for trout.

So it behooves any bass angler, armed with a flyrod or any other type of gear, to know the spots where bass are found, then to fish these spots in the most effective manner. Lake and pond bass, for example, are found on the shorelines in early morning and again in late evening, those times when the water surface flattens out and any small disturbance in the water is highly noticeable. Now's the time to be there with a bass-weight flyrod and any one of a handful of topwater flyrod baits designed to create a bit of disturbance. The important thing is to get that bug on the water as soon after the last rise as possible. Put it right in the middle of the ring left by the fish's swirl, if possible, but *get it on the water quick*. Bass have a way of nabbing some surface morsel, then moving off in search of more prey, so the sooner you present your bait, the better off you'll be.

Let's say you're on a smallish smallmouth stream and although no bass have shown themselves, you have reason to believe the bass will feed if you can get a bait to them. Your supply of artificials draws a blank, and now what? Break off the fake, tie on a small, short-shank hook, and turn over rocks submerged under shallow water till you locate and corral a little black hellgrammite. Impale this dandy bass bait just behind its tough-skinned collar and use the flyrod to flip the bait into the foot of riffles where the ruffled water falls off into pool. Keep a slack line; bass usually take a hellgrammite lightly in their jaws, running a few feet with it before inhaling the entire morsel, including the hook. Once the run pauses, raise the rod tip and strike the fish, and *hold on!* Stream smallmouth have a way of showing their displeasure that has snapped more than one rod in two.

Or maybe it's early spring and the bass, although they're cruising the shorelines, have not quite begun to fan out to spawning beds. Again using that flyrod and maybe eight feet of stout leader material, tie on a tiny white jig, the kind that weighs no more than $\frac{1}{32}$ ounce and is dressed with material that undulates when worked through the water. Drop this bait several yards out from shore, retrieving it very slowly, just fast enough to keep it off bottom. You may take an occasional small bluegill this way, but you'll also attract enough bass to make the day interesting. Bass fooled on such a rig don't really smack the lure. Strikes are usually just light taps as the bass inhales the tiny jig. Also, remember to play that bass with patience and a light hand because small jigs have wire hooks that straighten too easily for the bass to be horsed ashore.

Another tactic is effective wherever you see minnows skipping across the surface, indicating bass are below and actively feeding

Midsummer is a fine time to go topwater for bigmouth bass. This brace of fish hit a shallow streamer on consecutive casts.

on baitfish. Tie on one of the white or off-white streamer flies available (the Grey Ghost comes to mind as a good pattern) and wet it thoroughly before casting to aid in making the fly sink a few inches. Then drop the lure near skipping minnows or where such action was last seen. Don't be shy with the retrieval; remember your streamer should imitate a minnow that knows it's being chased. Bass are catlike predators and just can't stand seeing a meal get away, so make that fly skitter through the water like a spooked bait-fish. I've sometimes had luck bringing the fly right up on top and streaking it back toward me as fast as I could strip line.

Strikes at such fast-moving baits are always dramatic because the bait and the bass are moving at a good clip and the bass wants to kill the minnow before it gets away. Don't be surprised if the bass sends spray in your face when it strikes; I've had it happen.

The next time you're on a lake or pond containing a large pad bed, try using one of the surface baits—a popper will do, or a rubber frog—with upturned hook. Drop this bait smartly atop the pad bed, let it rest a few moments, then skip it to the next pad. After a few such hops, drop the bait in one of the holes in the pads, letting it wiggle and come to rest there, like a frog that's safe from harm. Chances are a good bass has long since noted the disturbances your bait has caused, and has followed along under the pads awaiting just such a moment. Strikes at times like these are explosive because the bass wants to glom the frog before it swims to another pad and the security it offers. Keep a tight leader, and keep your rod tip up at an angle to the water because you'll need the rod's flexibility to counteract the vicious strike. You'll also need a stout leader to muscle the bass out of all those pad stems.

One last tip. When midsummer puts bass on the shorelines only during the hours of darkness, here's a way to make that flyrod pay off in spades. Tie on a rather heavy leader—15-pound test isn't too much—and add an easily cast topwater bait, such as a balsa popper with rubber legs clipped short for easy casting. Then measure about thirty feet of line from your reel and mark it, maybe with a few wraps of rubber band, and move a boat or canoe that distance offshore. Even though the night is black and you can't see as far as your shoes, the marker will put your casts right where you want them—close to shore. Night-patrolling bass strike heavily and it's amazing how many really nice bass you can take in a single evening this way. Battling even a mediocre bass on a flyrod at night out of a canoe should provide more than enough excitement to bring you back on another summer's night. The slosh and roll of a big bass night-feeding near shore should inspire any dedicated bass angler worth his flyrod and leader.

10

Live Bait for Bass

If I was faced with a life-or-death challenge to catch a really *big* bass, a fish so fat, heavy, and cavernous of mouth that no one could question its trophy qualifications, I'd go after that fish with live bait.

Why? Because undoubtedly I would be using the natural food fed upon by that big bass in its natural environment. Big Florida bass, the hogs of bassdom, regularly feed on big shiners, some as big as the palm of your hand. Really big smallmouth bass in Dale Hollow and other impoundments feed on large crayfish, eels, and baitfish, and that's what I'd use to fish these standout bass waters.

Okay, I can just hear all you bassboat–worm-rod people raising cain because someone suggests there's a better way to catch bass than the tried-and-true methods you grew up with. But wait a minute. I didn't say I'd use live bait to catch the *most* bass, just the *biggest* bass.

You see, I happen to believe that the best-engineered lure made can in no way compare with a properly rigged, lively bait creature. For all their plastic diving lips, filed hookeyes, and soft-bodied construction, artificial baits merely approach the natural live action of the creature they're designed to imitate; put the artificials in the water with the real thing and it's no contest.

I opt for live bait because the big bass I'm after didn't get to be so big by being dumb. Unless the fish lives in the most remote spot in this country, by the time I arrive to fish for it, that bass has al-

The hellgrammite, or larval stage of the dobsonfly, is a favorite food of most river bass and can be found under rocks in the riffles.

ready seen more lures and *types* of lures than I'll ever own, so the chances of my fooling that fish into moving its great bulk for any fake I might try are so small as not to be worth my time – or the fish's. So I have a choice. I can flail the water till my elbow throbs and the bass won't feed for at least twenty-four hours, or I can switch to live bait and get serious about catching that behemoth instead of just chucking hardware at it.

Guess I should add that, although the bass is referred to here as an "it," the fish is almost certainly a female. It's been my experience, and the experience of all other bass anglers I've spoken with, that all *big* bass are females, and that male fish seldom reach the five-pound class. So I trust you ladies will excuse me if I call the bass a *her*. That's not chauvinism, it's accuracy.

So I will go after that bass with some live creature on which the bass feeds. It stands to reason that the bait, whatever it is, must

be of a species native to the fish's habitat. I might do very well drift-
ing live hellgrammites for smallmouth in Michigan, but the same
bait in Florida would do little more than get my line wet. You've
got to match the bait to the water, and sometimes to the size of the
fish, as well.

Let's say the bass lives in the Midwest, in a lake known to contain emerald shiners, panfish, and suckers. I have the choice among
these three species as to the bait I choose. Same goes if I'm after
those famous monsters of Santee-Cooper in South Carolina, or
Florida's mossbacks. Which of the native baits is easiest to use and
to keep lively on a hook? Maybe one or more of the available natural
baits is either illegal, according to fish and game laws, or so hard to
obtain (or expensive) that the ends don't justify the means. All these
factors should be taken into consideration.

A favorite method of fishing live shiners in Florida, and especially in the fine bass waters of the Ocala National Forest, is to rig
a large shiner with a surprisingly small hook through both lips,
using no added weight and no bobber. The shiner is swung into
the water along the edges of floating water plants and allowed to
swim freely in under this canopy in a search for refuge. What the
shiner often finds under that natural cover is a hogmouth bass, just
hanging around under the shade, waiting for some dumb shiner to
come close enough to nab. And that's often what happens, often
enough to make this method standard fare for catching truly big
bass (ten pounds and up) from Ocala's clear waters.

Let's say you're after really big smallmouth bass in a deep, cold
lake known for its great bass. You can chuck jigs and eels and what-
have-you till you're blue in the face, but to snag a really big bronzeback, try this: Gather or purchase a few 3-inch softshell crayfish,
and make sure they remain lively. Rig a light spinning rod with 6-
pound line and just enough split shot to carry your bait to bottom
without an undue wait. Then add a No. 8 short-shank Mustad hook
and impale the crayfish, starting on the underside, through the base
of the tail, so the point of the hook rides up. This is important because most smallmouth lakes have more than their share of bottom
rocks and ledges and any other rigging method will get you hung
up too often.

Largemouth, Smallmouth, and Close Kin

Now cast that lively little crayfish well out over deep water, especially while your boat is over the shallows at the top of a point or ledge, and s-l-o-w-l-y move the bait up, over, and through the profusion of rocks and boulders lying along the submerged point. Keep the retrieve *slow*—slow enough to make the crayfish appear to move naturally as it seeks safety under all those rocks harboring big smallmouth bass. You won't have to guess when a nice big smallmouth inhales your crayfish because he'll very nearly take your arm out of joint when he hits, not to mention what your tackle will put up with between hooking and (if you're lucky) boating.

Midwestern largemouth bass, like bass anyplace, eat what's available. That was the story of a bass that weighed nearly ten pounds and for several years stood as Ohio's state record. An angler, not a bass fisherman at all but a panfisherman, was angling with some success in an old strip mine pond for bluegills. He had several on a stringer by his feet when the string of bluegills seemed to jump out of the water, accompanied by a tub-sized swirl where the last bluegill had been. He gaped and tried to swallow; a bass the size of which he'd never seen before had not only eaten one of his panfish, but had had the temerity to grab it right off a stringer tied at the angler's feet!

Quickly, and with shaky hands, the angler reeled in, broke off his panfish hook and tied on a heavy steel hook he used to catch snapping turtles. A plump bluegill from his stringer provided the bait and the entire rig was lobbed into the pond to await further developments.

They weren't long in coming. First, the line moved sideways a few feet, then tightened as the eager bass chased, caught, and mouthed the luckless bluegill. When he was sure the bait was well within the lunker's maw, the angler struck hard and was solidly into his prize. The big bass was subsequently landed and the man had himself a state record specimen.

Outlandishly lucky? Maybe. But it illustrates that truly big bass feed often on the natural foods found in their home waters, and wise is the fisherman who takes the hint and offers native fare.

In spring, when lake and pond waters have not yet reached the minimum temperature needed to spur bass to spawn, there's a live

Talk about a stringer of hawgs! All of these fish hit live nightcrawlers fished on bottom in early spring.

bait that can be a real killer for big bass. In fact this bait seems to work better on big bass than on smaller ones—why, I don't know.

Spring lizards, also called salamanders, are egg-eaters. They have been known to invade the shoreline nests of bass and gobble the eggs, and big bass just seem to hate them. Have a look at how a bass nabs a salamander and you'll see what I mean. A bass takes a minnow or a frog with gusto, but the creature is really just grabbed in the fish's jaws, not brutalized. But let a salamander wiggle past a spring bass's nose and it's a different ballgame. The bass not only charges the salamander, it crushes it between jaws that grind back and forth, perhaps even shoving the creature into bottom mud in its fury to see the creature dead. Is it possible that a bass remembers from season to season what a salamander does to its clutch of eggs?

I think so. How else can the fish's vicious attack on these creatures be explained? Salamanders are slow-moving and certainly any bass in the lake could catch them at will—and often do.

So, wise is the early spring angler who knows all this and takes advantage. You'll need some live salamanders, which can be purchased at some live-bait shops, tropical fish stores, etc. Hook the sally through its lips, being careful to keep the point of the hook well away from its brain and bringing the hook point all the way out of the bait for secure hooking. Then, making sure your sliding bullet sinker above the bait moves freely on the line, toss the bait a minimum of twenty feet offshore, letting it settle all the way to the bottom on a *slack* line. Slack is the secret here; bass often grab a sally bait while it falls free to the bottom. Don't worry about detecting the strike, as the bass's method of mashing the sally will give you all the notice you need. If there's no strike during the freefall, let the bait rest on bottom for a full half minute, then hop the bait very slowly back toward you. A good way to do this is to thumb the reel spool, retrieving no more than three inches of line at a time while keeping your eye on the line where it enters the water. Remember, the wild salamander is not a fast-moving creature; it swims and crawls along the bottom, stopping now and then to hide under a rock or to inspect crevices for food. Your sally bait should appear to do the same thing.

Another live bait for early spring, either just before or during the spawn, is the popular and productive nightcrawler. And here I'm talking about the real jumbos, at least six inches long while at rest and at least as large in diameter as your little finger. What you want is a worm large, hardy, and lively enough to remain enticing for several casts, even though a heavy bass hook (short shank No. 6) is piercing its body in several places. Also, the large size of the bait helps in casting because spring-fished nightcrawlers are fished with

This angler cools his feet in an Arkansas river while tossing live crayfish downstream for bass feeding in the pool below. (Photo courtesy U. S. Forest Service)

Trophy largemouth bass hit plastic worms on the backwater ponds and scenic river waters near Punta Gorda Isles on Florida's west coast.

no weight other than that of their own bodies.

Trout anglers who fish worms tell us to hook the bait just once, through the collar. Not so for bass. I like to start with the worm's collar, then loop it around the hook shank a couple of times, hooking it again for added security and leaving at least three inches of the worm's tail hanging free to wiggle in a natural manner. But the hook is buried in a blob of worm, and this is what the bass grabs.

Down-home bass fishermen on many of Kentucky's fine impoundments fish live worms in this manner, often replacing rods and reels with long, limber cane poles at least fifteen feet in length and rigged with about five feet of 15-pound linen or monofilament

This angler is asking to get a treble hook impaled in his fingers. Bass this size should be netted or hauled aboard by means of a leader. (Photo courtesy Wisconsin Conservation Department)

line on the end. No reel is used. The boat, usually a cartop V-bottom or johnboat, is sculled along the muddy shorelines and the worm bait is vertically presented in, around, and over every stump, log and other debris studding the shore waters. The idea is to all but lower the bait into the bass's mouth. This is especially crucial in early spring when lake waters are colored with mud (bass can't see very far) and the water reading is low (the bass won't go far for a meal). So you have to almost tap them on the noggin to get them to hit. But the vertical-fishing method just described allows you to do just that.

When a bass takes the worm, he doesn't fool around. Whether

the bait is a single 'crawler or a whole blob of three or more, the bigmouth inhales the bait, hook and all. And remember, that bass is *already* in cover, so don't fool around trying to play it. The long pole lets you lift the fish, or at least horse it, right away from the stump it's under. If you're using the long pole, you just bring the pole in hand over hand, then grab the fish. If you're using a rod and reel, now's the time to slack off a little and subdue the fish by tiring it. But by all means get that sucker away from cover *right now* or he'll break you off as sure as little green apples.

Some things in this old world are surefire. One is that a surprising number of bass—damned *good* bass, too—will be caught by fishermen with no intention of taking bass. These people are on the water either for some other specific species—panfish, catfish, or whatever—or just generically *fishing* because they enjoy the sport. And most of these chaps are using live bait and *still* catch bass, bass that hit catalpa worms intended for bluegills, little minnows meant for perch, or hardshell crayfish fished deep for channel cats or bullheads. In my humble opinion, all this means that bass aren't so tough to catch after all—I've taken them on a thumb-sized hunk of *weiner*, for Pete's sake! Bass are suckers for live bait, even bait fished in the wrong manner on the wrong tackle and at the wrong time of year. And if this doesn't get your brain juices flowing the next time you go out after bass, well, turn in your favorite bass rod and take up bird watching, fella—you're hopeless.

Section IV

Special
Techniques

11

Fishing the Weather Fronts

The knock on my door interrupted the drumming of rain from a midsummer rainstorm that had begun only minutes before. When I opened the door I was greeted by the sight of two very wet but very happy fishermen. They were readers of the newspaper outdoor column I wrote at that time and couldn't wait to show off the string of bass they'd just caught from a local bass river. I pulled on a slicker, grabbed a camera, and braved the rain to look at the fish in their pickup.

They climbed into the truck bed under their camper shell, reached into an old metal washtub kept there for the purpose, and hefted the finest string of largemouth and smallmouth black bass I'd ever seen from that locally famous bass river. There wasn't a bass on the string of less than two pounds, and the heaviest largemouth weighed at least five pounds, easily twice the river's average where smallmouth usually dominate in both size and numbers. The anglers, dripping wet though they were, were obviously very proud of their string, and rightly so.

Not that it was anything too unusual for this pair. Far from it,

A dandy string of smallmouth from Tennessee's fine bass rivers. Catches like this are common in early spring and fall.

in fact, for they had something of a reputation for taking dandy messes of bass, but only at certain times, it seemed, and only when the weather was changing and unsettled.

They explained it this way: The movement into the river's area of a weather front, particularly in midsummer when the thermometer goes up and the bass catches go down, causes the bass to move, become active, and go back to feeding, which they abandoned when the water heated up and the dissolved oxygen content went down. Maybe it has something to do with the change in barometric pressure (although many so-called authorities on bass and bass fishing will tell you a falling barometer is the worst possible time to catch good bass). Perhaps the first sprinklings of rain freshen the stream water or lake water, causing the fish to awaken; or maybe a good hard rain washes a fresh food supply into the water, putting bass on the feed for as long as the new conditions persist. Whatever the reason, getting on the water when the weather is changing from one type to another works for these two, and it can work for you as well.

The two men keep an eye peeled on cloud formations, and take care to note the approach of forecasted rainstorms during the summer and early fall. As soon as the weather front appears imminent, they grab their rain gear and jump in the pickup that already holds all the bass gear they'll need. A cartop boat and small outboard kicker are strapped to the bed of the truck under the camping shell.

By the time their boat is on the water and moving slowly along good bass cover, the first few drops of rain dimple the surface. Instead of opting for the usual light bass gear of open-bail spinning rods and light lures, the men go in the other direction and use worm-weight baitcasting outfits, line testing about 17 pounds, and snap swivels holding crankbaits of about half an ounce apiece. Instead of fishing the obvious spots, the places flogged to a froth by other

Sometimes submerged points hold good bass and are wadable for the cautious angler. It's a good idea to question local fishermen about the whereabouts of such hotspots. (Photo courtesy Michigan Department of Conservation)

A handsome quintet of largemouth from a large reservoir. The fish all hit a deep-fished spoon-porkrind bait and were caught during a persistent drizzle.

anglers, these two stick to proven bottom structure for their top catches.

Rock shelves falling off over clay bottoms are their favorites. The big plugs are tossed well up into the shallow water, then cranked back at a good pace so that their oversized diving lips cause the plugs to dig deep, often ticking the rock and clay bottom on the way back, kicking up clouds of clay and maybe making small sounds as the plugs bounce off rocks and other debris.

Does all this suggest to you what natural bass food the choice of lure and retrieve might seem to imitate? You bet—crayfish, pure and simple. The casts into shallow water and the retrieves into the depths parallel the natural path taken by crayfish when chased by bass in the shoreline water, and the deep retrieves that kick up clouds of silt and clay also imitate a spooked crayfish in a hurry to find cover before he's gobbled up. Even the pace of the retrieves—as fast as the level-wind reels can be cranked—looks to a bass like a crayfish that's already on the move, and this accounts for the ferocious strikes this method brings. The bass—even the relatively small two-pounders—really nail the crankbaits, the men report. No soft takers these—the plugs are smashed hard enough that the fish most often hook themselves.

The theory is that these bass are *already* cruising the shallows and obviously feeding by the time the two anglers get on the water. Maybe yesterday's hot, sultry weather kept the bass in the depths and off their feed, but once the weather pattern changes noticeably, the bass go back on their feed with a vengeance, actively searching for crayfish and willing to hit any hefty bait that comes their way.

Let's take a minute to look at the bait these fish feed on. Crayfish usually enter the shallows several times a year to shed their outer shell (exoskeleton, technically speaking, a sort of outer skeleton that both protects them and gives them form) as their body grows and becomes too large for the old shell. At such times—up to four times a year in most parts of the country—the crayfish (or crawdad if you prefer) is particularly vulnerable to attack. No longer beneath a protective rock somewhere below the riffles, he is right out in the open in water thin enough to permit attack not only by the bass, but by raccoons, herons, mink, and a myriad of other creatures. Yet the crayfish must go to the shallows to spawn the new shell, and bass have no compunctions about taking advantage. Neither should the knowledgeable bass angler.

The onslaught of wet weather—be it a mere midsummer shower or a real frog-choker of a downpour—makes other bass food creatures more active as well. Amphibians such as frogs seem to move more when their land habitat is damp, perhaps because the extra moisture is comfortable on the frog's sensitive skin. Salamanders are of course moisture-sensitive and often make themselves more

The Tennessee River at Florence, Alabama, doesn't look very bassy, but local anglers have the whoppers to prove this is a fine smallmouth hotspot in spring and fall.

available to bass by entering the water at such times. This is especially true when bass spawn because sallys are great egg-eaters (see Chapter 10, "Live Bait for Bass"). Minnows, always a great bass bait in either lake or stream, may move more during or after a rain because the rainstorm makes more microscopic food morsels available and the minnows, like the bass that feed on them, take advantage by stepping up their eating habits for a short period. In the case of truly huge bass—like the bucketmouth 12-pounders found in much of the Deep South's top lunker lakes such as Kissimmee in Florida—even the increased activity of young waterfowl is of interest because there's no law against bass taking the odd duckling if and when the opportunity paddles by.

Weather fronts of any kind are worth trying for lake and pond bass. These men ply the lake for largemouth bass although a dusting of snow covers the trees beyond.

Midwinter fishing can produce good bass angling if you find pods of fish, and provided you dress warmly.

Let's assume, however, that you want to try for some bass and a weather front isn't forecast soon. Don't stay home and wait for something to happen, get out and *make* it happen.

If the weather's been hot and the barometer high for an extended period, you're going to have to work for every decent bass you catch. Sure, the little fellows will come easy and often, but if you're like me you'd rather take a single five-pound bass than its weight equivalent in runt fish, so let's concentrate on good bass in bad weather.

It's been my experience that during hot, humid weather, I find bass most often in pods, or loose schools, than at any other time of year. It's not that bass particularly like each other's company – bass are not social fish, by and large – but rather that the best possible water conditions (temperature, pH factors, oxygen, etc.) exist only in a rather small area, and the bass congregate there. The fish aren't spawning, are not actively feeding; they are just sort of hanging out until conditions improve and they can once again spread out over their range to feed. It's as if the entire bass population is in neutral, and this is a tough nut to crack if you're out to catch good bass. All the fish seem to have come down with lockjaw and a total lack of hunger and aggressiveness.

So what *will* make these fish hit? Annoyance; being bugged over and over and over until—faced with ever more irritating stimulations—they simply *have* to chase and strike a bait, if only to end the annoyance of its swimming back and forth, up and down, virtually right under their upturned noses.

And how do you find such pods of bass in hot weather? By knowing what creates the small areas of ideal conditions that they seek. Oxygen, a livable level of acidity versus alkalinity, perhaps a submerged spring that cools the water temperature for a few feet in every direction, maybe even a submerged current moving along an old riverbed, creek, or rock shelf—in other words, structure.

And once you locate these bass, how do you get them to hit? By putting that bait right under their noses, time and time again. The best artificial I've found for this job is a rather heavy metal wobbling spoon tipped with six inches of black or white porkrind. This bait casts accurately, doesn't need an extended retrieve to achieve full action, and can be fished vertically if the pod of fish is small and positioned in a tight spot, such as a brushpile or tight stream bend that won't allow a normal, flat retrieve. The new curl-tailed plastic grubs on a half-ounce jig head are also good for this chore, and will sometimes take more fish when jigged straight up and down than will the spoon-porkrind combination.

Either of these baits, by the way, are what I call *pure sinkers*—drop either into the water and all they want to do is sink. This is important for me because, like a great many other bass nuts, I tend not to fish deep enough long enough, even when logic tells me the fish are 'way down there and the only way to catch them is to fish where the bass are. I love a topwater strike about as much as anyone else and maybe that's why I have to force myself to fish deep. But if the bass won't hit anything except a deep-fished lure, I have no other choice but to follow suit.

When late summer gives way to autumn and the first frost cools the water, I make an almost total change in the lures I throw at bass. Away go the lures of the super-slow crawling retrieve and out come the baits that move with a faster pace because the newly cooled bass waters make the fish more active and willing to chase a fast-moving lure. Maybe bass somehow know that winter's not long in

coming and they feel the need to eat more in preparation. In any event, autumn finds me using more metal-bodied spinners, minnow-imitating lures such as the Rapala and A.C. Shiner, and fewer baits that imitate frogs, snakes, and other such midsummer bass delicacies.

Of course I'll have to alter my tackle a bit to accommodate the fast-paced lures. For speed in baitcasting gear I favor the Ambassadeur 5500C reel, the gray-colored little beauty with the speedy gear ratio of 4.7:1, nearly five spool revolutions for every crank of the handles. I'll use a longer baitcasting rod in autumn, too. It not only makes it easier to toss lures, since the rod tip has some flex and therefore makes repeated casting easier on the wrist, but it also lets me feel the action of a lure better than a shorter worm-type rod.

I also prefer slightly lighter lines. Still monofilament, of course, but now testing somewhere between 10 and 14 pounds instead of midsummer's 17 or 20. The new super-limp mono lines on the market are well-nigh perfect for tossing light lures without tangling, by the way.

Fishing the weather fronts—be they the quick changes wrought by midsummer rains or the more gradual cooling caused by autumn —can pay off big when you understand what these changes mean to the bass and how best to take advantage of the situation.

12

Night Bass Fishing

Night fishing for bass isn't much like the daytime sport we all do so much of. During darkness you can't see where you're casting, can't see the swirls of feeding bass, very often can't even see your hand in front of your face.

But what you can't see, you can *hear*. They say that blind people develop levels of hearing unknown to sighted people—it's as if they can't see the grass but they can hear it growing. Nighttime bass anglers approach this level of hearing, or at least seem to, because the sounds you hear at night on bass water seem magnified and amplified, and so do the bass on the other end of that line.

Take, for example, that midnight on a bass lake when I literally begged my fishing partner not to let me lose the bass that was even then trying to tie a knot in the anchor rope, using my gossamer 12-pound line as if it provided no drag at all. I'd tossed a topwater bait well back against a carpet of lily pads and chugged it back toward the boat when something huge went SPLOOOSH! and all of a sudden I was fast to a real hawg of a bigmouth. At first the fish jumped twice—sounding as if someone had dropped two suitcases

Morning and evening often find bass most active, so don't confine your fishing to the hot midday hours.

Be sure to use that landing net gently because a quick stab with the net can spook your fish and cause it to extend the fight.

into the lake when she hit the water full force and sideways. Then came a long, powerful run when the big fish shook its red-gilled head back and forth, trying to tear out the treble hooks and break the line too. At this point I admonished my fishing buddy that he must not, at all costs, be laggard in getting our small net around that fish for surely it was another state record, which at that time stood at about 11 pounds.

Slowly, far more slowly than I would have wished, I was able to winch the bass closer to the boat until finally the mesh of the little net closed around it and I was able to breathe normally for the first time in many minutes. I snapped on a flashlight and in its glow we guesstimated the largemouth hanging from that net at about seven pounds, maybe a little more, easily the best bass of the season thus far. But when the cold light of day made an accurate weighing of the trophy possible, the fish barely tipped the scales at five pounds.

So it is at night on a bass lake. Sounds aren't the only things that seem bigger than life. So do the bass themselves.

Beaches like this also can be fished at night with good success. (Photo courtesy U. S. Forest Service)

Bass, for all their predatory instincts, remain shy creatures that are easily spooked by a nearby disturbance. They also remain cold-blooded animals that draw their comfort—or discomfort—from the water around them. So it stands to reason that bass, particularly largemouth bass in ponds, lakes, and reservoirs, are most active at night, when darkness protects them, daytime winds and temperatures decrease, and when the darkness itself makes the still-shy bass brave enough to enter shallow water in search of food. At such times bass feed on virtually anything small enough to fit in their cavernous maws—frogs, baby muskrats, ducklings, insects, worms, snakes, crayfish, minnows, panfish, even the fry of their own species.

This preference for night is as true on the big, speedboat-scourged lakes as it is on the protected bass waters. Daytime activity on these huge impoundments very often keeps the poor bass near bottom with their heads tucked under the densest cover they can find while overhead the skiboats and super-souped bass boats roar up and down the channel. Swimmers pummel the water along sand beaches, sailors ply the quieter stretches, and sometimes high winds put whitecaps on exposed pieces of the lake. All this is well and good for vacationers, but bass and bass anglers stay clear until things settle down, and that means at night.

Sand beaches are great places to look for bass at night, after the boats and swimmers and hullabaloo have departed. Bass roam these beaches at night in search of food, as well as the very home docks of all those boats that ravage the lake during the day. Dock pilings and the like are great places to fish topwater plugs at night, especially those docks that are dimly lighted and thereby draw flying insects that fall to the lake and draw panfish and bass alike.

There are a few equipment changes you can make to help when you fish for bass at night and they all have to do with keeping things

Most bass anglers think of night fishing in connection with largemouths, but small-mouths, too, can be taken consistently at night, even on small streams. Here, a nighttime angler plays one at a productive bend in a little Pennsylvania creek.

Without illumination, night fishing can be awkward, even hazardous, when the time comes to unhook a fish, switch rigs, or unravel a tangle. This angler is using a battery-powered lantern. For safety's sake, a boat should also have running lights—a legal requirement on most waters for boats operated at night.

quiet. For starters, wear soft-soled shoes when afloat, such as tennis or gym shoes. Also, glue a piece of inner-tube rubber to the bottom of your tackle box to keep it from banging against the boat hull every time you want a new lure. You can also wrap the oarlocks in rubber or cloth to muzzle their squeaks and groans, and you can make sure that the anchor is attached with a rope instead of a chain to further lessen sounds on the water. You can also glue six-inch, rectangular squares of styrofoam to the inside gunwales of the boat near both angler positions. These are very handy places to temporarily store those baits you think you'll use; the trebles are merely imbedded in the styrofoam until the lure is needed.

Night vision is not to be underrated, either. Your eyes can see surprisingly well at night, once they become adapted to the dark and your pupils dilate as much as possible. And once you have good night vision, don't ruin it by shining a bright flashlight around the boat—or into your buddy's face, because he won't appreciate it. If you must carry a light, use one of those small pen-sized pocket flashlights that produce a bright-enough light to be useful, but not so much that the glow will blind you or, worse yet, spill over the lake and put down spooky, night-feeding bass.

On the subject of bass and light at night, I'd suggest you choose the darkest night possible for bass fishing. While it's been proven beyond doubt that bass don't much care whether they live in bright or dim light—all the magazine articles to the contrary—they *can* be spooked by sudden, bright light on a dark night. I remember a night when the bass were so active it sounded as though a herd of cattle was slopping around out on the lake. It was an overcast night and black as a coal bin. Then an unfortunate opening in the clouds let bright moonlight strike the water and this shut off the fishing as if with a switch. I've had heat lightning at night do the same thing —stop the bass immediately, as if on cue.

Finally, because you're out there in the dark and every bass you hang feels like a new world's record, you (and I) tend to horse the fish boatward sooner than we're supposed to. That not only risks losing the fish to a breakoff, it also threatens to put sharp hooks in unwary fingers because we're trying to land a bass that isn't tired and is fully capable of making that last lunge right at boatside. Tire that fish *first*.

Don't be afraid to go submarine at night, even though topwater fishing is more fun. If the bass aren't feeding on top, you'll catch far more by sending a bait down where the fish are.

I've used nine-inch plastic worms with occasionally great success at night, fishing them exactly as they would be fished during the day. Of course this requires extra-fine feel to know when a pickup occurs, when to let the fish run, and when to strike. Try this: Make your cast and let the worm settle to bottom. Wait a half minute, then, using just the tip of the thumb on your reel hand, turn the spool one-quarter revolution at a time toward you. This method will move the worm at the slowest and steadiest possible pace, making it easy for a bass to sense and locate it; and because your thumb is on the spool virtually all of the time, you should have no trouble detecting the lightest tap indicating a pickup.

Fishing for bass at night is really special when the summer insects hum and the real hawgs come up shallow to feed on frogs and such. Be there when this happens, brother, because it's like no other excitement in this wonderful world of bass fishing.

Section V

What the Experts Say

13

A Classic Lesson in Bass

If you could sit behind a pro bass fisherman for seventy-two hours as I have, watching everything he did, you'd be a better bass fisherman. No doubt about it. That's because pro bassers are successful only by being good. They encounter the same problems you do, but they often deal with problems differently, more completely, rather than merely hanging it up to wait for a better day. There is no "better day" on the tournament trail – it's either produce *right now*, or not at all.

I've had the good fortune to attend quite a number of bass tournaments, mostly as an observer. I made it my business, as a member of the outdoor press, to watch exactly what the contestants did under varying circumstances. So let's take a good, hard look at how the pro bassers go about locating, enticing, and catching bass, and see if we can't learn something of value.

Ricky Green, a native of Arkadelphia, Arkansas, is a seasoned pro angler. He has attended several of the biggest tournaments and won his share of both the money and the glory that victory brings.

Drift fishing below large hydroelectric dams means getting your bait well down into manmade currents where the big bass lurk. Only wide, stable boats are fit for this duty.

I spent time in the front of Green's bassboat, in one of the Classic tourneys put on by the Bass Anglers Sportsmen Society, and the first thing I learned about Green was his utter and complete dedication to winning. What did this mean in terms of Green's performance, and what can you learn from it?

Dedication to Green meant shutting out *all* else except locating, stimulating, and catching bass. He didn't chat during our long day on the water. He didn't even comment when cold rain chilled us or the noon hour brought hunger pangs that, for him, went ignored while there was fishing time remaining. He kept his selection of artificial lures wet all day long, trying this, trying that, swapping lures and techniques until one of the combinations caught fish, then sticking with it until it played out and he had to change again.

We were fishing tough Percy Priest Lake, Tennessee. It was tough weather for a fishing tournament: A cold front had brought falling temperatures and barometer, a chilling wind, and generally miserable weather. Any other bass angler would have headed for the dock and hot coffee, but not Green. He stayed on the water and not only kept looking for fish, but kept catching them as well.

In the first place, Green had used the two practice days to full advantage. He already knew many of Percy Priest's most important structures from studying a topo map, then searching the actual locations out with the boat and sonar unit. So when he went for all the marbles, he already knew precisely where to look for bass. He knew, for example, that if the bass weren't to be found along sharp dropoffs between shallow and deep water, perhaps they would be found along weedy shorelines, submerged fencelines, or other types of cover. In short, Green's pre-tourney research had located a variety of cover types, all there for him to fish if the situation required it.

When rough, cold weather descends on a bass lake, who would think the bass would congregate along a shallow clay shoreline? Not you and not me, perhaps, but Green knew of such a spot and we hit it just as the noon hour was making my stomach growl. Green refused the sandwich I offered him, not taking his eyes off the water except to tie on a favorite shallow-water lure of his, a Spider spinnerbait with a large chartreuse skirt over a single hook. I munched on a dry sandwich, watching Green, the fishing machine, in action.

A good bass caught on a spoonplug has this angler pleased.

He moved the boat about thirty yards off the near end of the clay shoreline, positioning the boat so he could move right up the shoreline by using only his trolling motor. His first cast touched down within a foot of dry land, and immediately Green bucked the rod tip vertically and started the heavy lure back to the boat, buzzing it on the surface with its oversized droplet spinner all aflutter. The bait hadn't traveled eight feet when a middle-sized bass swirled and took it. Green wasted no time on sporting niceties, however, virtually planing the three-pounder to boatside where he swung it aboard. It flopped on the floorboards, came unhooked, and I livewelled it while Green moved the boat slightly ahead as he continued to cast. Three more casts using the same buzz method nailed another bass, this one slightly smaller, and again I put it in the livewell with no word from Green. There were bass to be caught; no time for chatter.

Bass prefer to hang out around cover, so the smart angler concentrates his casts near logs, dropoffs, weedbeds, and other fish-attracting objects. The experts tend to keep their casts relatively short, say, thirty feet or so, but right on target to the prime spots. (Photo courtesy Michigan Travel Commission)

The shoreline had yielded a total of three bass by the time Green's Spider bait had crisscrossed all of it, and what the angler did then made me sit up and take notice, not to mention notes. He switched to a slightly smaller, black-skirted spinnerbait, turned the boat around and went down the same 50-yard shoreline, catching two more bass from the same water.

It was easily the most impressive bit of bass know-how that I've witnessed, before or since that day. But Green, never one to talk much during a tournament, explained his actions with wonderful understatement: "It turned cool here just a day or two ago, and the water hasn't had time to chill yet. I figured the bass had to be there." The other tip I learned that day is also worth remembering: Go back over the same water with a new lure of differing size and color, and you can sometimes catch bass where there supposedly aren't any.

By watching Green, as well as dozens of other competitors over the years, I've learned that I can cover more water, particularly when casting to shore from a slowly moving boat, by making a number of *short* casts rather than a fewer number of longer efforts. Pros I've watched—and fished with—kept their casts to an average of, say, thirty feet or less when working along an established line (shoreline, sunken roadway, or the like). Their casts were always right on target, too—nibbling at the edges of the weedbed, penetrating the holes in a sunken deadfall, closely paralleling the structure of a drowned creekbed or old road. By keeping their casts short, they were able to make them more accurate, and one of them told me that he was able to make as many as three short casts for every long effort he might have tried. You might not want to fish this hard, particularly if bass fishing is for you a relaxation and not a contest, but certainly there's something to be said for paring down your efforts for maximum efficiency. Heck, we'd all like to catch the most bass with the least effort, wouldn't we?

Very often, the professional anglers don't have time to go looking for pods or schools of bass because tourney time restrictions make it unwise to do a great deal of looking when *catching* is the only thing that counts. You and I, however, frequently have the time to look for lots of fish, rather than just strays. The important thing is to know enough about bass, and how they interact with habitat and weather, to be able to find numbers of fish.

I was amazed, for example, that Green was able to predict bass along a shallow shoreline after a cold front had moved through. I would have thought the fish would flee to deeper water where conditions supposedly would be more comfortable for the fish. But Green, having already tried several types of structure and location, had a pretty good idea that he'd find bass along that shore, and find them he did.

But such a prediction, while appearing impressive, may not be all that tough. Just think about it a minute. Let's say it's a bright, hot July day with high barometric pressure. The lake you're on offers both shallow and deep water. Where would you look for the fish? The most obvious answer, perhaps, would be the deeper waters, but what about dissolved oxygen, something the bass must have to survive, yet something that is often depleted in large impoundments in midsummer. Take a look at your topo map and see if one or more creeks or rivers enter the lake, then extend that line into the lake somewhat and check the depths found there. A creekbed should be indicated on the topo map, if it's a good one, along with the water depths. A spot such as this is likely to offer a number of tipoffs to schooled bass: deep, cool water; underwater structure (the creekbed itself); and a source of highly oxygenated water (the creek's flow). Now all you have to do is visit the location and start plumbing the depths with some deep-running lures—crankbaits, porkrind spoons, spinnerbaits, jig and eel, or perhaps a plastic worm rigged with a bullet sinker. If the bass are there—and everything indicates they should be—you'll limit out in a hurry.

Sometimes it's even less complicated to predict where the bass will be. I fish a smallish pond for bigmouths several times a summer. The pond is vodka-clear, unusual in my part of the country, and the bass are as skittish as big brown trout. They like to hang out in spots with some sort of overhead cover, such as overhanging willow branches, fallen logs, etc., almost anything that offers some cover and a bit of shade. Knowing this makes it easy to spot my casts alongside these natural fish-holders, and more often than

Knowing how to fish riprap can mean good catches of bass.

not I've been rewarded with half a dozen largemouths on nearly the same number of casts.

In fact, let me add one tip to the above situation. For some reason that as yet escapes me, one bait in particular seems to catch bass for me from clear water when all others fail. This is simply a quarter-ounce black jig, with or without hook dressing, with the addition of a black Curlytail. This all-black bait—easily cast which aids accuracy—can be tossed literally next to, on top of, and even beyond fish cover without hanging up, and the bass just love it. The bait is so compact it can be handled on either baitcasting or spin outfits, cast into a wind, and even replaced from time to time at very little cost. The black jig-and-Curlytail has been my ace in the hole for some time now. Give it a try.

Another tip I picked up from watching and fishing with the

pros was their diligence in fishing riprap. This is particularly true when smallmouths are the quarry, undoubtedly because these great gamefish are suckers for crayfish, and these little crustaceans are found in and around rock riprap dams, abutments, and the like.

The riprap structures most often drop gradually from the surface to depths sometimes exceeding fifty feet, depending on the size of the dam. Big smallmouths hang out here to gorge on the easily available food, and because the deep waters nearby offer protection and cover. Several of the pros I've fished with kept their boat well off the riprap and, using outfits that could handle long casts, dropped sinking or crank-down lures in the shallows, retrieving them right down the face of the riprap. As the baits dug deeper and deeper, they remained near the rock face, where the bass were, and these anglers caught bass.

Exactly which lures catch these riprap smallmouths seems to depend mostly on whether they get deep and stay there. I've seen big bronzebacks taken on tiny jig-and-eel combinations, plastic crayfish, small black or natural worms rigged with two single hooks, crankbaits with oversized diving lips, and several other baits, all of which went deep.

The pros most often used the sinking lures—jig combinations and worms in particular—to bounce off and drag along the sunken riprap face, probing the holes and creases left when the riprap construction was completed. It seemed, in this situation, that the bass were extremely reluctant to move far from the riprap to strike a bait, no matter how appealing. I think this is because the fish are used to finding crayfish and other creatures right along the riprap face, or no more than a foot or so away from it. Duplicating this natural situation—available food right on the rock wall—would be your best bet to score.

I'd advise, however, that you show more care than I did when you catch a nice smallmouth off a riprap wall. I was fishing, as a press observer, with an entry from Mississippi in a B.A.S.S. Classic in Tennessee. The weather was foul and the poor chap in the front of the boat could not catch the first fish, no matter how many lures he tried in a dozen different techniques. We were moving along the face of a riprap, which dropped off gradually to deeper water,

Bass tournaments, such as this one at Indiana's Lake Monroe, have been popular for years and offer thousands of dollars in prize money. Even if you don't compete, talking with contestants can teach you a lot.

with my partner casting toward the shallows and me snaking an occasional attempt into the depths. I remember I was using a skinny little Dardevle spoon with a porkrind trailer, letting it sink all the way to the riprap before slowly retrieving it up the rock face. Well, a three-pound smallmouth nearly took the rod from my hands when it struck the spoon, and my troubles weren't over when I'd brought the bass aboard. The contestant took one long, angry look at the bass, swore at length under his breath, and went back to casting, never to speak to me again during the long hours of that fishing day. I'm sure he thought I'd caught the bass he was after, and he was angry over it. Yet he'd been fishing the shallows while I plumbed the depths. Sometimes it works out that way, even if the silence for the remainder of the day was a little hard to take. And so was another writer's 3½-pound smallmouth, taken the same day. It robbed me of the daily $50 prize for the best writer-caught bass. Ah well....

At virtually every multi-day bass tournament I have attended, evening hours for the pros were spent preparing tackle for the next day and, more importantly, talking with each other about the sport they so dearly love. Being competitors, of course, meant that they didn't reveal to each other where the bass were or were not—it was every angler for himself or herself—but the talk was 100 percent about bass and bass fishing, and there is a lesson in this for those of us who have yet to become tourney-class.

Hang around the avid bass anglers. Attend your local bass tournaments, even if you don't enter. Rub elbows with the guys when they come off the water, maybe buy one of them a beer or a soft drink. Chances are he will be more than willing to talk about bassing with you, since bass are most important to the both of you. Compare the tackle he uses, and how he uses it, with the outfits you take fishing. Perhaps he's made a few tiny but important changes in his lures, which in turn alter the action just a bit. How does he rig his plastic worms, and has he had any success with the relatively new worm rig calling for the use of a swivel 18 inches above the hook? How does he rig his boat for bass angling? Does he use a pH meter, and if so, how does he interpret the readings?

All of these questions and more can come up in casual conversation, but don't be surprised if the competitor turns the tables and asks about your methods as well. Remember, his experience, his innovations, and his successes have limits just as yours do, and if he can learn from you, he'll be a better bass fisherman for having made the effort. So swap information every chance you get. That's how the pros stay on top of their game.

14

Bassing Tips from the Experts

There are countless bass of all species caught in the United States every year. The actual number probably runs into the millions, and in bassing, as in all other kinds of fishing, it's true that ninety percent of the fish are caught by ten percent of the fishermen. Why? Because these people know what they're doing, they apply a few basic bits of knowledge to their fishing, and they try harder than the average angler.

These so-called experts aren't necessarily tournament anglers, although they easily could be. They're merely people who love to fish for bass, but they also love to *catch* bass, and so they see to it that they do things right every time out.

Let's look at a few of the things these successful fishermen do — and don't do — to put weight into their livewells on most every fishing trip. Maybe we can learn something.

Fish, Fish, Fish

Once you learn to ride a bicycle, they say you never really forget how, but this certainly isn't true when you fish for bass. The more you fish the better you get, and therefore the more fish you'll catch.

Let's say you average five bass every time you fish. If you doubled the number of times you fish, would you then catch ten bass

169

The more you fish—whenever and wherever you can—the better your fishing skills will become, and the more fish you will catch.

per trip? Twenty, perhaps? Or perhaps you fish an average of fifteen times a season and average a seasonal catch of forty-five to fifty bass. If you doubled the number of times on the water, would you then catch perhaps 100 fish a season? Nope. More likely, that number would have ballooned to 500, maybe even 800 fish per year. Why? Because you're using your skills as an angler much more often, shortening the time between on-the-water sessions, so to speak, and you will just naturally both retain what you already know and learn new skills, new techniques, as the season progresses.

Take something simple like fishing knots, for example. I know that I tie much more effective knots when I fish a lot, if only because I am doing it more often. It's darn frustrating to have a knot fail just when you've got that lunker at boatside, ready to thumb, and this happens far less often when you've tied the knots so often and so well that knot failure just doesn't happen any more. (See Appendix B for a review of the most useful bass-fishing knots.)

Homer Circle, *Sports Afield*'s Angling Editor and a fine bass angler, did some research into knots and determined through exhaustive testing that knots tied dry, rather than with line moistened with saliva, proved to be up to fifteen percent stronger than their

By learning to read streams, you'll be able to detect where the bass are and know how to present that lure or bait most effectively.

wet-tied counterparts, perhaps because knots tied wet draw up on themselves so very tightly that the monofilament wraps tend to crimp one another, weakening the overall test of the line-knot combination. Keep this in mind the next time you knot that worm or crankbait to your bassing line.

Familiar skills are performed best. This means that you'll operate your trolling motor, outboard, free-spool reel, and a dozen other things better the more you use them. Maybe you've fished with a guide or fishing buddy of long experience and watched him lay out effortless and accurate casts time after time, all the while maneuvering his bassboat with one foot on the trolling motor controls. Watching people like this always reminds me of a well-machined piece of equipment—smooth, effortless, productive. Your friend got that way by spending a *lot* of time learning his skills,

When you take off for a day's fishing, don't skimp on the tackle, else you may miss out on unexpected opportunities.

and chances are he catches more bass than the average chap who ventures out after bass only a few times every summer.

Of course, the more often you fish for bass, the more territory you'll cover and the more bass hideouts you'll uncover. If you make an honest effort to locate bass every time on the water, it just has to be true that you'll end up locating more lunkers if you fish more often. Combine that search with the use of a good topo map and the aid of an underwater sonar outfit to determine structure, and before long you'll know where most major fish hideouts are located, and you can fish them accordingly.

Let's not forget patterns here, either. The more you fish, the more you'll begin to recognize certain patterns about the bass's locations and preferences. Let's say one overcast morning you catch five bass off one clay shoreline that never produced bass for

Trolling is not often seen among bass anglers, but it's a good way to cover a lot of likely water.

you before. It occurs to you that something must have put those bass on the shoreline, and you think perhaps it was the overcast morning with its low-light conditions and the shallow water. So, in an effort to prove the theory, you move to another shallow clay

shoreline and, hotdamn, you take three more bass. You now have caught eight bass from a formerly-barren type of habitat, and you file that away for future use.

This kind of thing can happen only if you fish often enough to establish the pattern and get to know the water well. This in itself is reason enough to fish, fish, fish as often as you possibly can. It is a simple fact that the more you fish for bass, the more bass you'll catch. You can put that in the bank.

A Variety of Tackle

In the many bass tournaments I've attended I couldn't help but notice the variety of rods and reels and lines used by the serious tourney angler. Nearly every tournament boat I looked into carried at least two, sometimes as many as four, types of terminal outfits. Most often there was a baitcasting outfit, a medium-weight open-bail spin rig, an ultralight spinning or spincast rig, and, in a few cases, a fully rigged flyrod, plus a full complement of lures and accessories for each outfit.

You may not want to invest in all of this stuff, or even lug all of it along on every trip, but such a variety of tackle does give you the greatest opportunity to take bass regardless of their location or bait preference.

I recall a bass tourney on Lake Mead a few years ago. Mead's waters are very clear, and the competitors soon discovered that the fish were refusing all normal presentations while demanding very light tackle, gossamer lines, and tiny lures. Only those anglers equipped to provide these caught bass. The others got skunked; even though many of them later reported seeing bass in the clear waters, they had no success in getting the fish to take bait.

Most serious bass fishermen, even if they don't compete in

Going where the fish are isn't always easy. These anglers head for some of Florida's more remote largemouth waters. (Photo courtesy Florida News Bureau, Department of Commerce)

tournaments, own more than one rod and reel, so why not make that second, or even third, outfit one that will do something for you that the others won't do? Carry a free-spool baitcasting rig for worms, spoons, and the heavier plugs; a spin outfit for light crankbaits, pork baits and the like; and maybe a fly outfit for those times when bass are in thin, clear water and hitting on surface insects or minnows.

There have been times when I wished I'd brought the right tackle along, like that evening on East Fork Creek some time ago when the smallmouths were smashing anything that dimpled the surface. The bass rejected all subsurface baits, shunning my best efforts to take them on diving minnow imitations, spinners, even small plastic worms. So I had to improvise. I tied a very light, sensitive balsawood bait on a loop in my ultralight line and dropped the little plug at the head of East Fork's little pools. As the plug drifted downstream, I twitched it ever so little, just enough to send telltale ripples across the quiet surface. The smallmouths loved it, smacking the little wooden fake as though it were a live insect or struggling minnow or frog. By nightfall I'd caught over a dozen smallmouths, the smallest of which went nearly two and one-half pounds and the best fish weighing nearly five pounds. If I could do that with improvised gear, what would I have caught with a bass-weight flyrod and a handful of hairbugs or poppers? And how much more fun would those bass have been on a long wand instead of a spinning outfit? To this day I wished I'd had the right rod along, but at least times like that have taught me never to determine what the fish want ahead of time—I now let the bass do the determining.

Go Where They Are

A countrified friend of mine says that if you want to catch a frog you

Where both occur (and such places are many), bass and bluegills compete for available food and cover. It's a good idea to remove several pounds of both each season in order to maintain the overall health of a pond.

A light craft can put you next to bass that otherwise would never see a lure. This angler uses a Coleman Scanoe.

have to look where there are frogs, and while that sounds a bit self-evident, the principle behind it certainly applies to bass fishing.

In a word, fish the hot lakes, and don't waste time anywhere else. There is a new reservoir of about 10,000 acres not too far from my home that is only about three years old, and it contains plenty of bass in the 1½- to 2-pound range. I can fish there for half a day and catch a couple dozen of these little fellows with no problem.

But I also know about, and have permission to fish, a series of three large farm ponds just a bit farther from home than the reservoir. The ponds are several years older than the reservoir, and the bass they contain are more mature and considerably larger. So you already know where I'm spending my time these days—on those ponds catching bigger bass, and I'll continue to do just that until the bassing there falls off drastically.

That doesn't mean I've forgotten all about the reservoir and its plentiful, if small, bass populations. Because about the time the ponds peak out and the fishing there begins to fall off, which I believe will happen in another three years or so, the reservoir will have matured enough to begin producing lunkers of its own. And since I already know the reservoir contains many bass, I can look forward to taking not only good-sized fish, but plenty of them, a few years down the road. As it happens, I've fished the reservoir enough already to know where the hotspots are likely to be, so I should be able to familiarize myself with the reservoir's layout with only a couple of trips on the water. The reservoir is my ace in the hole when the ponds play out, and it feels good to know I can look forward to good fishing for years to come.

Fishing the hotspots also means finding locations within existing waters that, for one or more reasons, suddenly start to produce fish where few or none were caught before. This can be intentionally or accidentally made to happen. For example, local fishing clubs can build and sink fish attractors to create crappie feeding stations, and this in turn will attract and hold bass as these predators begin to feed on minnows attracted by the brushpiles. Or perhaps an existing lake has been expanded into terrain covered with standing timber, fallen logs, an old roadbed, or whatever. Newly flooded lands are always very attractive to bass because they offer a sudden bonanza of creatures to eat—insects, frogs, snakes, tadpoles, etc. The bass go prowling these new areas for food, and the wise anglers, knowing this, make it their business to be there, rods and reels in hand.

A lake I fish a great deal was expanded in this manner a few years ago, adding some 500 acres to the impoundment and flooding a woods of dead and standing timber. For a while immediately after the expansion, it seemed as if every bass in the lake had moved into the new area, and for two full seasons the new hotspot produced stringers of bass worth taking pictures of. Now that the bass population and distribution have stabilized somewhat, bass are once again caught lakewide. But that still-new area continues to be the top producer, probably because the bass that found good living there hung on as permanent residents.

Finally, let's not forget the hundreds of new impoundments created every year by highway departments all across the country. Remember all those ponds and small lakes you noted right alongside the newer interstate highways? They got there because the highway contractor needed fill dirt to use for his roadbed. He made arrangements with nearby private landowners (farmers, usually) to remove the needed fill for the highway in return for creating one or more ponds, usually to the landowner's specifications. The new hole in the ground filled with creek or ground water, and soon another bass pond was born. Many state fish and game departments will stock these new waters with fingerling bass and panfish in exchange for the owner's assurance to permit some public fishing access. Within four years after such small impoundments have been stocked, good fish begin to show up for those lucky enough to know about these ponds, and who get permission to fish them from the farmer. By the way, a dandy way to make sure you're invited back to fish another time is to offer that farmer, your host, a few fresh bass fillets at day's end. He'll appreciate your thoughtfulness, and that goes a long way toward keeping your favorite bass plugs wet trip after trip. And of course you respect his wishes about keeping gates closed, respecting livestock, and calling ahead for fishing permission. It's *his* land, after all.

The Positive Bass Fisherman

It's important to be positive, especially when you go after bass, because these finny battlers are not easy to find nor are they easy to catch. There will be days when you can't seem to catch the first bass, and during such times only a positive attitude will keep you

In spring, fish the fast water just below dams and overflows because this is where migrating bass will congregate.

on the lake and trying.

Whenever I drive by a piece of water suspected of holding bass, whether it's a lake, pond, or stream, I can't help but slow the car a bit and look over the situation. A slow eddy of current curls behind a fallen log, creating a perfect place to drop a spinnerbait or perhaps a jig and eel. A riffle falls off into a fan of slowing water and there, by the grace of God, a well-presented hairbug should catch a smallmouth or two. And what about that row of cottonwoods overhanging the water? I'll bet there are summer evenings when bass go nuts over insects falling into the water from those trees.

I think like a bass, and so should you. Get into the habit of

looking beyond the surface of the water, much as a deer hunter trains himself to look *into* a woodlot or thicket, and not just at the surface of it.

Once you get the hang of recognizing bass water when you see it, you won't have to hope there are fish there when you fish it. You'll *know* they are there. I've had many tournament anglers tell me the hardest part about bass fishing is finding the bass to begin with. "Once I've found 'em, getting 'em to hit usually isn't hard," Ricky Green explained one day when we shared a tourney boat. The very same thing applies to positive thinking: You *will* find the fish, and you *will* discover which bait and which presentation will take them.

Positive thinking can do wonders for the weight of your stringer come day's end. Say you've been on the water all morning, with only a runt or two to show for it. You've already tried all your favorite lures and the usually productive places, and turned up zilch. You look at your watch and almost decide to call it a day and go in for lunch and a siesta. But on the way to the dock you spy a spot that somehow you haven't fished before, and so you turn in that direction and give it a whirl. Maybe you catch bass from the new spot and maybe you don't. What's important is that you're adding to your knowledge of that piece of water, knowledge that can be applied later. Maybe that new spot contains heavy weeds all across the mouth of a small inlet, and although it doesn't produce for you now, nearing midday in a bright sun, you file it away and try again in the evening when the light level is reduced. The bass move over those submerged weeds to feed with the coming of evening, you show up and begin tossing a plastic worm or maybe a topwater bait and *wham*, you're into another hotspot.

Wading permits the angler to work productive waters closely, putting his lure into every spot that may hold fish.

Epilogue

I Just Called Him Mule

"Now *that's* a smallmouth!"

These were Pete Tally's words the first time he saw the fish I had dubbed Mule. The big fellow had shouldered three small rock-bass against the rocky shore of Indiana's Whitewater River, backed off for a running start, and grabbed all three in a swirl that measured six feet from edge to edge. Pete and I had been in the middle of a float trip down twelve miles of the river, innocently plugging for bass, when the monster bronzeback made his dramatic display of gorging on the hapless redeyes. Pete couldn't believe his eyes.

"There isn't a fish in this river big enough to move water like that," Pete mumbled, still staring at the ring of froth the bass had left as a calling card. "Not in the whole state. He'd go three feet if he went an inch."

I had seen this particular bass three times before, and had the shattered nerves to prove it. The first time was six years earlier when I still lived in Cincinnati and fished the Whitewater often with Jerry Sarver. Jerry's family and mine shared the same apartment building, and we used to strap his aluminum johnboat on his

This scrappy smallmouth hit a white spinner in a cold Michigan lake. (Photo courtesy Michigan Travel Commission)

bright red station wagon and spend long, lazy days on the river's current after bass.

Jerry had floated the river several times before, but that particular day was my first on the water and I asked Jerry what type of gear I should bring.

"Mostly you'll use medium spinning tackle with plastic worms, spinners, and small plugs. These fish don't usually weigh more than three pounds, so you won't need anything too heavy. Unless," he added without smiling, "you tie into that big buster down on Buzzard Bend."

I knew Jerry well enough by then, or thought I did, to suspect he was pulling my leg about any extra-big fish in the river. After all, there was and is nothing unusual about the Whitewater. Counting all three forks, the river has about 200 miles of water moving at an average of six miles per hour. It has a total drainage area of 1,500 square miles, and courses over some of the finest examples of fossils in this part of the world. But a monster smallmouth? It didn't seem likely.

The trip went well enough in the morning. We hung about twelve bass, all of them smallmouth, and we strung half that many to take home. It was during a shoreline lunch that the subject of the big bass came up again.

"You *were* just pulling my leg back there, weren't you?" I asked, half hoping he'd 'fess up and admit he was pulling my leg. "I mean, there really isn't any hawg smallmouth in here, is there?"

"Well," Jerry began, crushing his cigarette on a handy slab of limestone. "I could tell you about the time I had two rods broken in the same summer by that fish. Or about how he straightened out a set of trebles on a muskie spoon last October, but I know right now there's no way you'd believe me. So rather than be called a liar, I'll put you into where that fella lives and, if he's at home, you'll see for yourself." Jerry is a man of his word, and if he said he could put me over that bass, then that's the way it would be.

It took us another hour to float downstream to where Buzzard Bend makes its S-curve below towering clay bluffs. Jerry had named the spot because of the huge number of turkey vultures that came to wash their feathers in the river flats every summer morning. We approached the run of fast water leading into the pool, and Jerry said I'd better get rigged if I wanted a shot at the bass.

My partner wasn't too happy that all I had in the boat was a standard spinning rod and 12-pound line on an open-faced reel, but it would have to do. For bait Jerry dug out a large silver minnow-like plug, shaped like a cigar with a big plastic diving lip on the front. He handed it to me and indicated that I should tie it on.

"Now this bass doesn't hang out around a log or other structure," Jerry said. "He just lays right out there in the current, right on bottom, and waits for food to come swimming by. You might have to cast it by him six times, but that seventh time he might hit. And if he does," he said without smiling, "may God have mercy on your soul."

Well, being a normal kind of bass nut, I was pretty psyched up by that time. I like to get into big fish as well as anybody, so you'll understand why that first cast was a little shaky and somewhat short of the mark. I cranked the bail shut and hurried the oversized silver minnow back to the boat, lifting it from the water just over the gunwale.

"He came up to have a look, but you'll have to get it down deeper if he's going to take it," Jerry said, bending from the waist and looking into the pool. He noticed my blank look and explained.

"You were so busy getting that plug back you forgot to look where it came from," he said pointing. "The bass floated up under the bait and watched it back to the boat. Now make this cast dig the water a bit more."

The oversized minnow, which I figured to weigh at least a full ounce and a half, plopped into the river and wiggled out of sight as I began to retrieve. The tip of my rod made little nodding motions as the plastic lip bit deeper into the pool, and then the line started going the other way, as if a slow but determined train had snagged a treble and was late getting out of the station. By the time I realized I had a fish on, he was already on his way to the surface.

What followed looked more like a rodeo than a bass battle. That fish was out of the water so much I could make out the scars along his midline. He didn't thrash or froth the pool, but just bucked and crowhopped like some ornery pack mule determined to get rid of whatever he'd been strapped under.

"Ride him, cowboy!" shouted Jerry, leaning back on the oars to keep us in deep water. "Don't let him throw you yet!"

Well, when it happened I didn't have much to say about it. The bass bucked right out from under those trebles and threw the plug back so hard it clanked off the aluminum gunwales hard enough to leave a dent. The last we saw of him was a ragged tailfin following his heavy body into the deepest water in Buzzard Bend. Jerry rowed us downriver to the car, and neither one of us wet another line all afternoon. There are some things which command reverence, and that brief battle had been one of them.

The second time I saw Mule (I'd already named him because of the way he bucked away my minnow) was two years later, in early June, when the bass were spawning all up and down the Whitewater. This time I was wading with Mike France, and we'd hiked in about two miles from the road to fish Buzzard Bend. We didn't hang Mule that trip, but what we saw was enough to make a true believer of Mike.

We were using fly tackle, pulling big streamer flies over the bass beds and hooking the papa bass whenever they thought our fake panfish were after their eggs. Mike stopped to watch a fat two-pounder circle his nest a few times, and was about to whip his streamer a bit upstream when he suddenly dropped his gear, rod and all, right in the river. I stopped fishing and asked what the Sam Hill he was doing.

All he could do for a minute was point.

"There was this big fish..." he stammered, his sunken tackle forgotten. "The bass just scooted off his nest, like he was gonna chase something, and...and got eaten by the biggest damn smallmouth I've ever seen. He was this long," Mike muttered, stretching his hands apart about a yard.

Then we heard a heavy splash and turned just in time to see

Smallmouth and spotted bass water at its best. Although small, this little woodland stream holds bass up to four pounds. (Photo courtesy Little Miami, Inc.)

How big is your dream bass? Here are two dandies that didn't get away. (Photo courtesy Bass Anglers Sportsmen Society)

Mule make that weird bucking motion on the back side of the pool, the tail of Mike's papa bass peeking from between his jaws. It was a good half hour before my compadre thought to retrieve his fly rod, and another fifteen minutes before he used it again. You'd have thought Mule had turned into some kind of sacred shrine, the way he had of making believers out of simple fishermen.

I Just Called Him Mule

I wasn't even fishing the third time I saw Mule. My newspaper had sent me to Brookville, Indiana, to look over a dam and reservoir the Corps of Engineers was building on the Whitewater, and one of the job foremen invited me to float downstream a bit so he could point out where the increased flow line would be, once the dam was in place.

We floated for an hour or so, the foreman pointing out water marks and seasonal levels and such, and me more or less just riding along and watching the scenery go by. Pretty soon we got down to Buzzard Bend, and suddenly the foreman perked up and started telling me how this part of the river would be completely different, once that fine new dam started grabbing river water.

"Of course, this pool won't be here any more when we get done," he said, swinging his hand in a wide arc across the pool. "The water will be about halfway up those bluffs over there, and we'll use earthmovers to take the bend out. It would slow the current too much, you see."

Oh, it was going to be grand, he told me. Twenty-two miles of slack reservoir, and a drowned river down below. Just what we needed, he said. And then Mule showed up.

I guess that fish must have aged a bit over the years, because he missed seeing our canoe and rammed us so hard the foreman nearly jumped out of his seat. But he wasn't hurt near as bad as Mule. The old fellow tried to dive, but floated back up till he was dry on one side, his raggedy tailfin waving weakly just under the surface. I could see his brown lateral line had picked up a few more grayish scars since the previous year, and one side of his lower jaw was ripped where he'd sacrificed a bit of hide to get away from some fisherman's trophy room. I could see he wouldn't be around for many more summers. Finally he got a little water under his tail and pushed himself out of sight.

Well, Pete Tally never did get to set his hooks into Mule, at least not that I ever heard of. He still talks about him once in awhile, but only to me, he says, because nobody else would believe him. I guess he's right enough; who would believe a monster smallmouth in a run-of-the-mill Indiana limestone river, anyway?

Appendix A

How to Fillet Bass

Everyone loves to catch bass, but there are regions where some anglers claim these fish are second-rate table fare at best. Supposedly, they have an undistinguished flavor by comparison with trout and other species, and occasionally they're described as having a "murky" taste. Maybe this is just as well, since it means more bass are released. But the fact is, bass are delicious when properly prepared. It's possible that an occasional fish may have a less than perfect flavor if it's been living in shallow, dank, weed-filled, murky water; but as a rule, the only part tainted by such imperfection is the skin. The solution, obviously, is to skin your bass rather than scale it. Bass have tougher hides than some other gamefish, anyway. Small ones can be very good if merely scaled and then crisp-fried, but the larger ones are best skinned regardless of the water they came from. Skinless bass fillets make great eating, so once you've caught your bass, just follow these illustrated instructions to fillet it expertly.

Always use a good knife, such as this super-sharp Rapala fillet knife with a flexible blade and safe scabbard.

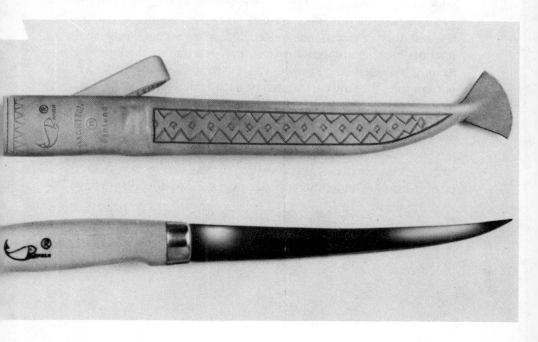

Start with a bass of any keeper size, and if possible, work on a hard wooden surface.

The first cut should be made directly behind the gill flap, cutting all the way down to the backbone.

Next, turn the blade's sharp edge toward the tail of the bass and start cutting towards the back.

Continue the cut right along the backbone, severing the ribs as you go.

Be sure to include all available meat in your cut. This is easily done if you'll take your time.

Don't sever the fillet completely, but keep a tab of skin attached at the back. Then flip the fillet so the meat-side is out and carefully separate the skin from the fillet, using a sawing motion of the blade.

Repeat with the other side of the fish and you have two bass fillets needing only to be trimmed free from the ribs.

No need for further directions at this point. Dig in!

Appendix B

Most Useful Knots for the Bass Fisherman

Here are twenty-two knots that are very popular among fishermen, and of course the reason they're popular is that they're excellent for their intended purposes—easy and fast to tie, not inclined to slip when subjected to tension, strong enough not to break easily when a lunker hits, and streamlined enough not to snag, interfere with the action of a bait or lure, or spook your quarry.

I've chosen these ties on the basis of their usefulness in bassing, even though they're all of value in many other kinds of angling. In some cases, I offer a choice of more than one knot for a given purpose. This may be because there are differences of opinion as to which is strongest or easiest to tie, or because each has some other advantage. For instance, the improved clinch is somewhat stronger than the turle, but a fly fisherman may sometimes prefer the turle because it lets a fly ride higher on the water. Above the instructions for tying each knot, I've listed the knot's intended use or uses so you can make the best selections for your tackle and fishing methods.

CLINCH KNOT
Used to fasten hook to leader or fly to tippet.

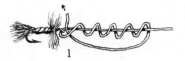 

Pass the end of the line through the eye of the hook or fly, and then form three or four twists around the standing part of the line. Pass the end through the opening between the eye and the beginning of the twists. Pull on the standing part of the line to tighten the knot. Tighten thoroughly and trim the end, but not too closely.

IMPROVED CLINCH KNOT
Used to fasten bait hooks, bass bugs, flies, or other lures to line or leader. Reduces line strength only slightly.

Pass the end of the line through the eye of the hook or lure, and then form at least five twists around the standing part of the line. Pass the end through the loop between the eye and the beginning of the twists, and then fold it back through the large loop formed in the previous step. Slowly pull on the standing part of the line, until the knot fits tightly up against the eye. Trim the end.

DOUBLE-LOOP CLINCH KNOT
Same uses as the improved clinch knot, but is stronger.

Follow instructions for improved clinch knot, except pass the end of the line through the eye *twice* at the beginning.

DOUBLE IMPROVED CLINCH KNOT
Same uses as the improved clinch knot, but is stronger.

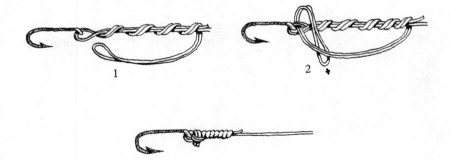

Follow instructions for improved clinch knot using double line throughout the tie.

REVERSE CLINCH KNOT

Used to snell a hook or to secure a single hook to monofilament line. A good knot for live-bait fishing.

Pass the end of the line through the eye of the hook and form a loop at the hook's bend. Then bring the end of the line back to the eye, and form three or four twists beginning near the eye and working forward to the bend. Pass the end through the loop, and tighten by pulling on the standing part of the line. Trim the end.

BLOOD KNOT

Used to join two lines of almost the same diameter, as when joining monofilament sections in making tapered fly leaders.

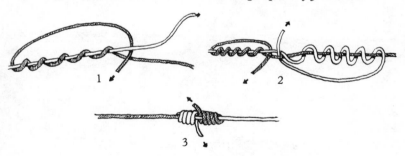

Wrap one strand around the other at least four times, and pass the end through the fork between the strands. Make the same number of turns with the second strand, but in the opposite direction, and run its end through the opening in the center of the knot, in the direction opposite that of the first strand. Hold the two ends and pull the standing part of both lines in opposite directions to tighten. (You can use your teeth to hold the ends.) Trim the ends. Leave one end 6 to 8 inches long if you want to tie on a dropper fly or sinker.

DOUBLE SURGEON'S KNOT

*Used to join two strands of unequal diameter, as when tying
leader to line or tying a tapered leader.*

Place one line parallel to the other, with the ends pointing in opposite directions. Use the two lines as a single strand and make a simple overhand knot, pulling both strands all the way through the loop; then make a second overhand twist through the loop. Holding both strands at each end, pull the knot tight. Trim the ends.

PERFECTION LOOP

Used to make a loop in the end of line or leader.

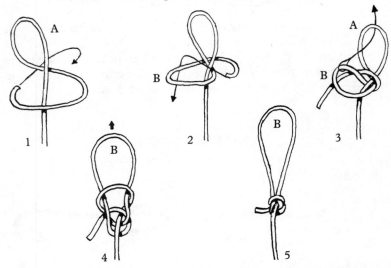

Make a loop (A) and hold the crossing point between the thumb and forefinger. Make a second loop (B) by bringing the end in front of and then around behind the crossing point; place the end between loops A and B. Pass loop B through loop A. Pull upward on loop B to tighten the knot, then trim the end.

PALOMAR KNOT
Used to join monofilament to swivels, snaps, hooks, or lures.

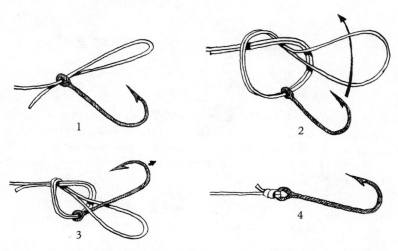

Slip a 3- to 5-inch loop through the eye, and make an overhand knot with the double-stranded loop, but do not tighten it. Holding the overhand knot with one hand, bring the loop over the hook or lure. Work the line to draw the loop to the top of the eye. Pull both the tag end and standing line to tighten the knot. Trim end about ⅛ inch from knot.

TRILENE KNOT
Same uses as the Palomar knot.

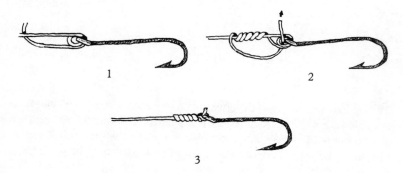

Pass end of the line through eye twice, and then make at least five turns around the standing part of the line. Run the end through the two loops between the eye and the beginning of the twists. Pull slowly on the standing part of the line until the knot fits snugly against the eye. Trim the end.

TURLE KNOT

Used to tie a fly to a tippet. Although not as strong as the improved clinch knot, the turle knot permits a fly to ride high on the surface of the water.

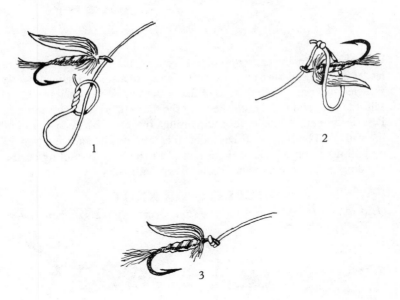

Pass the end of the leader through the eye toward the bend of the hook, and make a simple overhand knot around the standing part of the line to form a loop. Open the loop so it can fit around the fly, and place the loop around the neck of the fly, just behind the eye. Pull on the end of the leader to draw the loop tight around the neck. Pull on the standing part of the leader to tighten the knot. Trim the end.

NAIL KNOT

Used to join a leader to a fly line. This is the best knot for use with modern synthetic lines, but will cut the old silk fly line.

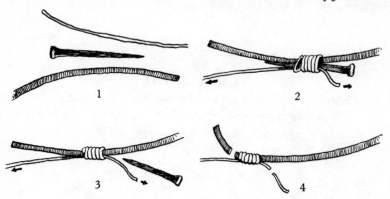

With the ends pointing in opposite directions, place the butt end of the leader and the end of the line along the length of a tapered nail, allowing sufficient overlap. Wrap the end of the leader five or six times around itself, the nail, and the fly line, keeping the loops up against one another. Pass the butt end of the leader back through the loops, between them and the nail. Pull both ends of the leader, then remove the nail, and tighten by pulling on both ends of the leader. Test the knot by pulling on the standing part of the line and leader. Trim both ends.

DOUBLE NAIL KNOT

Used to join leader sections of the same or nearly the same diameter.

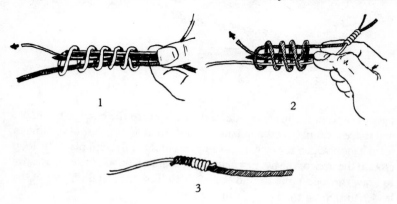

Follow instructions for nail knot to make the first knot, but tighten it only enough to prevent unraveling. Form a second knot, using the end of the other leader section, and tighten enough to prevent unraveling. After both knots are formed, pull slowly on the standing part of both leader sections until the knots come together and are tightened securely. Trim both ends.

DROPPER LOOP
Used to form a loop in a strand of monofilament.

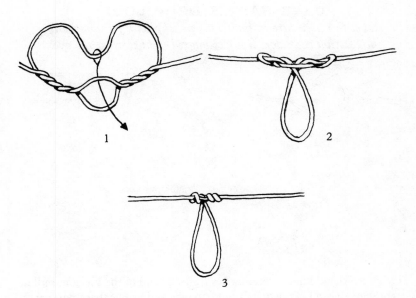

Make a loop in the line and wrap one end six or seven times around the standing part of the line. Pull the center of the loop between the turns, near the middle. Hold the loop with your finger to keep it from pulling out, and pull on both ends of the line to tighten the twists and secure the loop.

LOOP KNOT

Used to fasten lure to line.

Tie an overhand knot in line, leaving the loop loose and enough line below the loop to tie the rest of the knot. Pass the end through the eye and back through the loop of the first knot, and then tie a second overhand knot around the standing part of the line. Pull tight and trim.

DAVE HAWK'S DROP LOOP

Used to fasten lure to line. This nonslip loop permits more lure action than does a knot snugged tight against the eye.

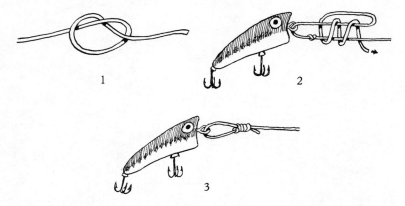

Tie an overhand knot several inches from the end of the line and pull it tight. Pass the end of the line through the eye and bring it back parallel to the standing part of the line. Then bend the end back toward the lure, make two turns around the double strands above the overhand knot, and pass the end through the loop formed when you turned it back toward the lure. Slowly draw the knot tight by pulling on the end, and pull on the lure so that the jam knot slides down to the overhand knot. Trim the end.

ALBRIGHT KNOT

*Used to join lines of different diameter, as when tying fly
line to leader or heavy leader to finer leader tippet.*

1

2

Make a long U in the end of the heavier line. Hold the lighter line parallel to the U, wrap it once around one leg of the U, and make about ten wraps around the standing part of the lighter line and both strands of the heavier, working *toward* the bottom of the U. Bring the end of the lighter line through the bottom of the U, and pull slowly and evenly on it until the knot is tight. Trim the ends.

The last five knots in this appendix are the bass fisherman's most important ties in the Uni-Knot System, a series of variations on a single, easy knot. Devised by Vic Dunaway, a famous angler, editor of *Florida Sportsman*, and author of numerous popular fishing books, the Uni-Knot System contains knots useful for all types of freshwater and saltwater fishing.

DUNAWAY TERMINAL TIE

Used to tie line to all types of terminal tackle.

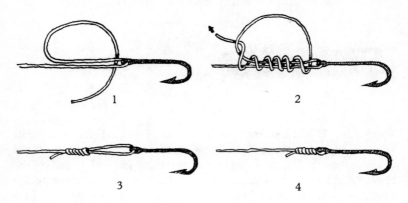

Pass at least 6 inches of line through the eye and bring it back parallel to the standing part of the line. Fold the end of the line in a circle toward the eye. Coil the end six times around the double line, and then pass the end through the circle. Holding the double line at the eye, pull the end to snug up the coils. (This is the basic Uni-Knot that is used in the other Dunaway knots described below.) Pull the standing part of the line to slide the knot against the eye, and continue pulling until the knot is tight. Trim the end.

DUNAWAY LOOP CONNECTION

Used to connect line to a lure so that it has free, natural action.
When a fish is hooked, the knot slides tight against the eye.

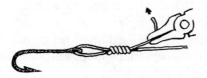

Follow instructions for the Dunaway terminal tie until the coils are snugged against the running line. Slide the knot toward the eye until the desired loop size is reached, and pull the tag end with pliers to tighten.

DUNAWAY LINE-JOINING KNOT

Used to join two lines of about the same diameter.

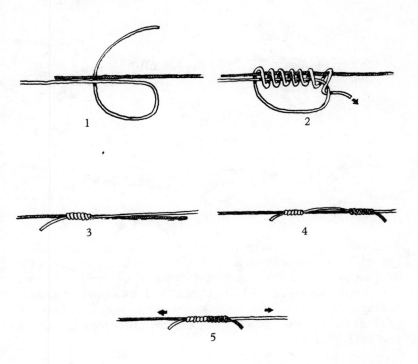

Place about 6 inches of the two lines parallel to each other, with the ends in opposite directions. Fold the end of one line back toward the middle of the overlap and tie the basic Uni-Knot, making six turns around the two lines. Pull the tag end to snug the knot. Tie another Uni-Knot using the loose end of the second line, and snug it in the same way. Pull the standing part of both lines in opposite directions to slide the two knots together tightly. Trim the ends close to the outermost coils.

DUNAWAY LEADER-TO-LINE KNOT
Used to connect a line to leader.

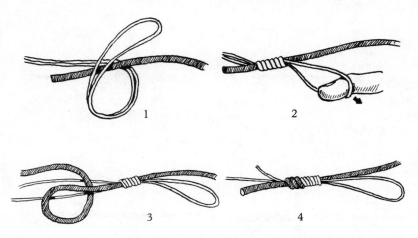

Form a long loop in the end of the line. Place about 6 inches of the doubled line and leader parallel, with the ends in opposite directions. Using the doubled line, make a Uni-Knot around the leader, using only *three* turns. Then use the loose end of the leader to tie a Uni-Knot around the doubled line, again making only *three* turns. Pull on the standing line and leader until the two knots are drawn tightly together. Trim the ends and the doubled loop of line.

DUNAWAY HOOK SNELL
Used to snell a hook to line or leader.

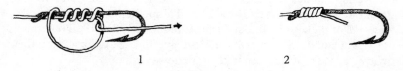

Run the line end through the eye for about 6 inches. Form a Uni-Knot circle back toward the eye and complete the knot, making as many turns as desired around the line and the hook shank. Pull on the end to close the knot. Pull on the standing line and hook to tighten it. Trim the end close to the coil.

Index